Treasures of St Andrews University l

Treasures of St Andrews University Library

Edited by Norman H. Reid
with
Marc Boulay, Rachel Hart, Elizabeth Henderson,
Moira Mackenzie and Maia Sheridan

ORBIS TERRAE COM

Quam ex Magna Vniuersali Gerardi Mercatoris Domino Richardo Gartho, Geographię ac cęterarum bonarum ar

Polus 90 Arcticus

AMERICA SIVE INDIA NOVA
Anno Dⁿ 1492 à Christophoro Columbo nomine Regis Castellę primum detecta

Circulus Arcticus

Tropicus Cancri

Circulus Aequinoctialis

Tropicus Capricorni

Circulus Antarcticus

Noua Guinea
nuper inuenta quę an sit insula an pars continentis australis incertum est.

Hanc continentem Australem nonnulli Magellanicam regionem ab ejus inuentore nuncupant

TERRA AUSTRALIS.

Archipelago di S. Lazaro

Archipelago minore

MAR DEL ZVR

EL MAR PACIFICO

Polus Antarcticus 90

Duysburgi Cliuorum

DIOSA DESCRIPTIO

fautori summo, in veteris amicitię ac familiaritatis memoriā Rumoldus Mercator fieri curabat A°. M.D.LXXXVII.

Cover image: historiated initial 'T' depicting St Andrew, excised from a missal (French, c.1500). ms38667

Endpapers: detail from page background of Treasure no. 48.

p.1: Library stamp

p.2: Aerial view of St Andrews with the mediaeval street layout still in evidence (anon., 2007).

pp.4–5: World map from G. Mercator, Atlas, sive cosmographicae meditations de fabrica mundi et fabricate figura. De novo multis in emendatus et appendice auctis studio J. Hondii *(Amsterdam, 1630). r17ff G1007.M3*

Opposite: North Street [St Andrews] looking west. Photograph by Thomas Rodger, c.1860. Albumen print from glass plate negative. ALB35-10

Treasures of St Andrews University Library

First published in 2010 by
Third Millennium Publishing Limited,
a subsidiary of Third Millennium Information Limited.

2–5 Benjamin Street
London
United Kingdom
EC1M 5QL
www.tmiltd.com

ISBN 978 1 906507 15 2

Edited by Norman H. Reid with Marc Boulay, Rachel Hart,
Elizabeth Henderson, Moira Mackenzie and Maia Sheridan
Designed by Susan Pugsley
Production by Bonnie Murray
Reprographics by Studio Fasoli, Italy
Printed by Gorenjski Tisk, Slovenia

Contents

Foreword

University members who pass daily through the archway into St Mary's College on their way to lectures, tutorials and laboratories rarely raise their heads to look at the inscription above them. Picked out in gold, in high-relief from their plain background, are the words IN PRINCIPIO ERAT VERBUM (In the beginning was the Word). It is hardly remarkable that our predecessors decided to write the opening line of St John's Gospel above the entrance to the university's School of Divinity but it is a useful exercise to consider what, beyond their immediately obvious theological interpretation, these words might be meant to convey to the generations of students and scholars who have passed, and continue to pass, beneath them.

All those who study here are heirs to a great tradition in which the written word and the quest for essential truths are intimately connected, with the former offering both a platform for setting out new ideas and a vehicle by which these ideas might be disseminated widely and accurately for approval, amendment or, not infrequently, rebuttal. In the Middle Ages, books were so valuable that they were sometimes chained to their shelves. Technological developments have changed the way many of us access the written word but have not lessened its importance. If many today no longer believe in the truth of the Word to which the Gospel author refers, there has been no corresponding loosening of the bond that exists between words and an individual's search, through academic endeavour, for truth.

I write this foreword as the University of St Andrews prepares to enter its seventh century of academic exploration. At the same time as we draw enormous strength from our rich intellectual heritage, we remain ever-conscious of the responsibility we bear to those who came before us – and those who will follow in our footsteps – to continue to enquire, to debate, to offer alternatives and new perspectives, and to embrace difficult questions.

The treasures that you will discover on the following pages are not limited to books. Rather you will have an opportunity to gain some sense of the rich depth and breadth of the University Library's priceless holdings. In very different ways, each item featured in this volume presents us with what Carlyle, speaking about books, referred to as 'the articulate audible voice of the past'. The several examples of photography included alongside mediaeval manuscripts, early printed books and official university documents bear witness to the past too, while inviting us to reflect on the sometimes tense, always-evolving relationship between word and image.

Scholars, staff and students at the University of St Andrews are extraordinarily privileged to have such precious resources to draw on as we make our own contributions to our academic community here in Scotland and beyond. I hope that this book will, in its turn, prove a source of inspiration and delight to its readers.

Louise Richardson
Principal and Vice-Chancellor

Venice. One of 24 watercolours by Joseph Axe Sleap (1808–59), pasted in to Thomas Moody's Journal of a tour through Switzerland and Italy, *1822. msD919.M7E22*

Preface

Come and take choice of all my library,
And so beguile thy sorrow …

(*Titus Andronicus*, IV.i.34)

It is an immense privilege to be associated with a great library; even more so to be entrusted with the care of its treasures. With collections rooted in the mediaeval traditions of faith and learning that put St Andrews at the heart of Scottish life for centuries, it has been suggested that the University Library can claim to be the oldest continuously functioning library in Scotland. Such a pedigree, of course, carries with it the dual responsibility for nurturing and protecting this panoply of riches and for ensuring that it can be accessed and appreciated by the widest possible audience. Consequently, whoever has an interest in using the Special Collections Department in St Andrews University Library is welcomed as a friend with a mutual interest.

The purpose of this book is to help broaden our audience, to share more widely the beautiful, the rare and the simply fascinating. Selecting a meagre 50 objects from over eight miles of shelving has been at once an invidious and an enthralling task. The aim was to provide multiple cross-sections of the holdings – from mediaeval to modern, arts and sciences, printed, manuscript and photographic, from the university's own archives as well as its gathered collections – and to bring these visually stunning items to new audiences using both illustrations and short, accessible, interpretative essays from acknowledged experts.

The 50 friends of the Special Collections Department who have written the essays have shown immense enthusiasm for the project. Each of them has a connection with St Andrews as staff, student or as visiting researcher. They have in common a love for the material they have described so eagerly and skilfully.

The selected items having defied any attempt to shoehorn them into a thematic organization, they are instead presented in an order dictated only by the authors' surnames. For ease of reading we have deliberately kept technical description and provenance information to a minimum. Summaries, not necessarily comprehensive, relating to provenance and custodial history are provided for each item, but any reader requiring further detail should contact the library. Dimensions are given, these being, for bound items, the size (height × width) of the leaf rather than the overall size of the binding. The catalogue or reference number of each item is also provided.

This book is testament to its contributors' ready willingness to participate, to meet demanding deadlines and to accept with good humour and generosity the scourge of the editorial pen. All of my colleagues in the Special Collections Department have readily devoted time and energy to the project, not least by keeping the ship afloat when some of us were too engrossed to fulfil our other duties.

Historiated initial and detail from leaf of a Bible (France, c.1280). ms38677

The editing of the book has been a joint effort: I am deeply indebted to Marc Boulay, Rachel Hart, Elizabeth Henderson, Moira Mackenzie and Maia Sheridan, who, as well as contributing essays, have all played a variety of vital roles throughout the project. The photography, integral to a work of this nature, has all been undertaken by Marc Boulay except in those few instances where otherwise credited. I am also grateful to David Roche, in the university's Print and Design unit, for his excellent scanning work. In the Principal's Office Peter Clark, Stephen Magee and Christopher Smith, and in the library Jon Purcell and Jeremy Upton have all been immensely supportive of the project, and I also wish to thank Louise Richardson, Principal and Vice-Chancellor of the university, both for her support and for the Foreword. Finally, I must record my appreciation of the friendly, patient and skilled assistance of Joel Burden, Susan Pugsley and the team at Third Millennium Publishing Ltd.

Inevitably, a book such as this has a concentration on the past: it is no coincidence that it is published as we anticipate celebrating 600 years of the University of St Andrews. In her introductory essay, however, Elizabeth Henderson points out that we must also celebrate the 'vibrant future' of the library. The collections are neither static nor entombed: they continue to grow in quantity and, more importantly, in stature and social value, as they are increasingly used and appreciated. We trust that their future promises to be every bit as exciting as their past.

Norman H. Reid
St Andrews, February 2010

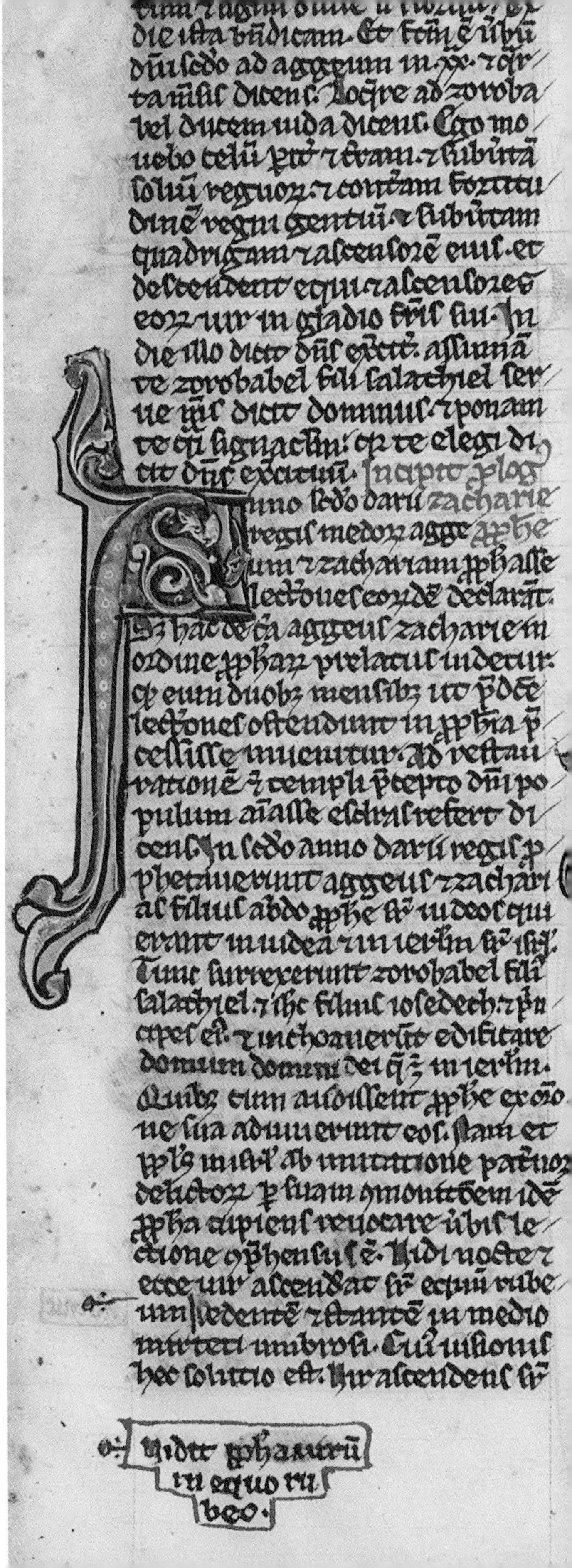

Contributors

(All University of St Andrews unless otherwise indicated)

Geneva Bible *(London [Amsterdam], 1599), bound with the* Psalms in the metrical version used in the Church of Scotland, *(Edinburgh, 1640). The red velvet chemise is sumptuously embroidered in gold and silver thread, and includes the emblem of the Wardlaw family, connected with Henry Wardlaw* (c. *1365–1440), bishop of St Andrews. Presented to the library in 2001 by Lady Hanbury-Tenison and Major Alastair J. Rennie. Bib BS170.C40*

Robert Bartlett, Professor of Mediaeval History
Marc Boulay, Photographic Archivist, Special Collections
Michael Brown, Reader in Scottish History
Margaret Connolly, Honorary Research Fellow in English
Alex D.D. Craik, Emeritus Professor of Applied Mathematics
Robert Crawford, Professor of Modern Scottish Literature
Robin D.A. Evetts, Senior Inspector of Historic Buildings, Historic Scotland
Duncan Forbes, Senior Curator of Photography, National Galleries of Scotland and Honorary Research Fellow, School of Art History
Luke Gartlan, Lecturer in Art History
Christine Gascoigne, former Head of Special Collections and former Acting Librarian
Christopher Given-Wilson, Professor of Late Mediaeval History
Philip Gribbon, former Lecturer in Physics, and former Honorary President, Mountaineering Club
John Haldane, Professor of Philosophy
Rachel Hart, Muniments Archivist, Special Collections
Elizabeth Henderson, Rare Books Librarian, Special Collections
Kay Redfield Jamison, Professor of Psychiatry, Johns Hopkins School of Medicine, and Honorary Professor, School of English
Chris Jones, Senior Lecturer in English Literature
Ann J. Kettle, Honorary Senior Lecturer in Mediaeval History
Antonia Laurence-Allen, School of Art History
Sara Lodge, Lecturer in English Literature
Julian Luxford, Senior Lecturer in Art History
John McCallum, Visiting Scholar, Reformation Studies Institute
Christine McGladdery, Teaching Fellow, St Andrews Institute of Scottish Historical Research
Moira Mackenzie, Head of Reader Services, Special Collections
Matthew McLean, Research Fellow, School of History
Alexander Marr, Lecturer in Art History
Paula Martin, Independent scholar, Fife
Roger Mason, Professor of Scottish History
P.G. Maxwell-Stuart, Honorary Lecturer in History
Lorna Milne, Professor of French
Martin Milner, Senior Lecturer in Biology
Robert Mitchell, Honorary Curator, St Andrews Botanic Garden
A.D. Morrison-Low, Principal Curator, Historic Scientific Instruments and Photography, National Museums Scotland
Steve Murdoch, Reader in Scottish History
Tom Normand, Senior Lecturer in Art History
Andrew Pettegree, Professor of History
Norman H. Reid, Head of Special Collections
Steven John Reid, Lecturer in History, University of Glasgow
Louise Richardson, Principal and Vice-Chancellor
Edmund F. Robertson, Professor of Mathematics
Nicholas Roe, Professor of English Literature
Larry J. Schaaf, Independent Scholar, Baltimore, Maryland
Maia Sheridan, Manuscripts Archivist, Special Collections
Robert Smart, former Keeper of Manuscripts and Muniments
Graham Smith, Emeritus Professor, School of Art History
T.C. Smout, Professor, Institute for Environmental History and Historiographer Royal in Scotland
Clive R. Sneddon, Institute of Mediaeval Studies
Thomas Traill, Professor of Medicine, Johns Hopkins School of Medicine
Kristin De Troyer, Professor of Old Testament/Hebrew Bible
Malcolm Walsby, Reformation Studies Institute
J. Tia Wheeler, School of History
Pat Willmer, Professor of Biology and Vice-Principal for Learning and Teaching
Isla Woodman, History of the Universities Project

St Andrews University Library

There was a library in St Andrews long before there was a university. The headland to the east of the town, still dominated by the ruins of the great cathedral, was an important site of ecclesiastical activity from at least the 8th century and of international pilgrimage from the 10th. No records survive of books owned by the early religious community, though the 15th-century chronicler Walter Bower mentions an early mediaeval gospel book with a silver cover. When Robert, bishop of St Andrews, founded an Augustinian priory at St Andrews in 1144 to serve the cathedral, he included in the endowment a gift of all his books. Shortly after Robert's death in 1159 work began on a new cathedral church, which would be the largest in Scotland, and the adjacent priory buildings were probably constructed

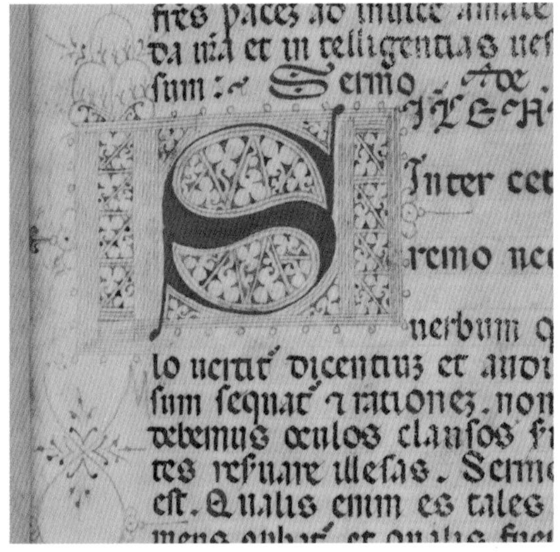

Initial from Pseudo-Augustine, Sermones ad fratres in eremo *(Italy, 14th century). msBR65.A9S2*

Right: mediaeval book presses in the cloister wall of St Andrews Cathedral.

Opposite page: the east gable of St Andrews Cathedral from the cloister.

in the 13th century. Typically for a monastery in this period, cupboards for storing books are built into the wall at the northeast corner of the cloister. Little information survives about the priory library, but when the compilers of the *Registrum Anglie*, a catalogue of selected books held by British ecclesiastical institutions, visited St Andrews near the end of the 13th century, they reported the titles of 95 texts that interested them. Twelve of these titles are found in one surviving late 12th-century manuscript codex (Treasure no. 44). This manuscript has evidence of an iron chain ring at the head of the front board, suggesting that the cathedral priory may have had a chained library.

St Andrews, then, had been a seat of learning for at least two centuries before the first tentative steps towards the foundation of a university took place. A group of scholars began teaching in St Andrews in 1410, although the papal bulls authorizing the granting of degrees were not issued until 1413 (no. 35). Teaching methods at mediaeval universities were primarily oral: prescribed texts and accompanying commentary were read out and

taken down by the students. The first known reference to the acquisition of books by the young university occurs in the minutes of the Faculty of Arts (no. 50): on 17 January 1416 it was agreed to send £5 from faculty funds to Paris to buy texts of Aristotle and commentaries on his logic and physics. Unfortunately, on 21 May 1416 the money was reallocated to help pay for the new faculty mace, and the purchase of books was postponed until more funds were available.

The College of St Salvator was founded by Bishop James Kennedy in 1450 on North Street, but an embryonic library was already developing on the south side of the town. A dedicated book-room at the university is mentioned in the record of the faculty meeting of 13 August 1456. It was decided that there should be a wooden lectern, on which library books could be secured, in a small room at the end of 'the big school'. This was presumably a room in what was known as the 'pedagogy' of the Faculty of Arts, endowed by Bishop Wardlaw in 1430 with lands on the south side of South Street, adjacent to the College of St John; the faculty had met in the College Chapel as early as 1416. A library on South Street has been a constant feature of the university ever since.

Gifts and bequests were the main sources of books for the new library. Two early graduates of the university made donations, including Aristotelian and pseudo-Aristotelian texts and a commentary on Aristotle's *Ethics* by Thomas Aquinas. A little later, in 1496, Alexander Inglis, dean of Dunkeld Cathedral and archdeacon of St Andrews, bequeathed 12 volumes, mainly classical texts, to the Faculty of Arts and the pedagogy. He left a printed Bible to the cathedral priory, but it is not now known whether the volumes for the university were manuscript or printed. Unlike Inglis's books, a number of volumes survive in the library's collections from the personal library of William Schevez, a graduate of the university who was bishop of St Andrews from 1478 until his death in 1497, and a scholar and bibliophile of international reputation. He may have bequeathed them to the priory, whence they later came into the university's collections via the library of St Leonard's College, founded within the priory precincts in 1512 initially for the education in arts and theology of Augustinian novices (no. 21). His books are now widely dispersed but are instantly recognizable by his bold and distinctive signature. His library is said to have been rich in scientific material, and he is credited with having encouraged the teaching of both geometry and astronomy in St Andrews.

After the Reformation an Act of Parliament of 1579 brought about the 'New Foundation' of the university, directing St Leonard's College and the 'auld college' of St Salvator to teach philosophy and arts, while the 'new college' of St Mary (founded in 1538 on the site of the older pedagogy) became a divinity college. An inventory headed *Bibliotheca Leonardina*, probably dating from the late 1590s, gives an indication of the college's books at the end of the 16th century. It lists 262 volumes, although it concludes 'thair ar sum ma buikis in the Librarie, quilk tyme culd not permitt to seik out'. It seems possible that groups of books in the St Leonard's inventory represent several donations, one of the most significant being that of James Stewart, half-brother of Mary Queen of Scots, lay commendator of the cathedral priory, earl of Moray and regent of Scotland. He appears to have given donations both in the late 1550s and after he became regent in 1567. Many of these books survive in the collections today (no. 23). This is evidence of sustained patronage which appears to span the Reformation crisis. The principals of the college, including George Buchanan (principal, 1566–70) (no. 26), were also

Signature of William Schevez, Archbishop of St Andrews, from a volume of six incunabula bound together. Typ NL.A85JT

Many of the books donated by Lord James Stewart are bound in this style. John Chrysostom, Opera *(Basel, 1530). Roy BR1720.C5*

generous donors of books. St Leonard's, then, which had already benefited from receipt of books both from the pre-Reformation priory library (including some of Schevez's collection) and the earlier collection held by the pedagogy (apparently including some of the late 15th-century donation of Alexander Inglis), appears to have maintained a tradition of benefaction, and by the late 16th century had amassed a considerable collection.

There is a recurring legend in St Andrews that the 'common' library of the university was built to house books bequeathed by Mary Queen of Scots. It is certainly true that in preparation for the birth of her son in June 1566 Mary recorded her wish to leave her Latin and Greek books to the University of St Andrews, to found a library there. However, although the queen's intention at this time is quite clear, it is also stated that these provisions were intended to apply only if both she and the child died. In the event, both Mary and her child, the future King James VI and I, survived and Mary's books remained in her possession. By the 1570s, when James VI's tutor Peter Young was endeavouring to recover those of Mary's books that had been dispersed since her abdication, he was clearly doing so as part of an effort to build a library for James.

In fact, the foundation of the University Library owes more to George Gledstanes, the archbishop of St Andrews and chancellor of the university, who received George Abbot (later to become the archbishop of Canterbury) on a visitation to assess the facilities of the university in 1608. They agreed that a common library was a necessity, and persuaded the king, himself a noted scholar, to lend his support to the foundation. In 1612 a gift of books was made in the name of the king – the Royal Collection – and in the same year Abbot himself made a further gift, including a copy of the 1611 first edition of the King James Bible. Other notable donations around this time included that of Patrick Young, the royal librarian, whose gift included

Portrait of James VI of Scotland and I of England by John de Critz (1604). Courtesy of the Scottish National Portrait Gallery.

Hieronymus Bock, De stirpium *(Strasburg, 1552), from the Wedderburn bequest. Wed QK41.B7*

a set of the Complutensian Polyglot Bible (no. 46) and a fine 15th-century printed copy of the *Quaestiones* on the 'Sentences' of Peter Lombard by the 14th-century Scottish philosopher John Duns Scotus (no. 13). James VI and I visited the university himself in 1617, and, noting that the building supposed to accommodate the library was as yet incomplete, he instructed that it be finished 'with all speed'. This may have been a source of irritation to the university authorities, since the instruction came without any money to enable this to happen. The building was substantially finished within a year or so, but it was a gift of the princely sum of £1,000 in 1642 by Alexander Henderson, a graduate of the university and noted theologian, which allowed it to be completed. This is the structure that still stands on South Street, with a panelled library above a meeting hall, known as Parliament Hall since it accommodated a meeting of the Scottish parliament in 1645–6.

Pen and wash drawing of the University Library c.1767, by John Oliphant. Gra DA890.S106

Further important 17th-century gifts of books were those of Sir John Scot of Scotstarvit (1585–1670, a 1605 graduate) and his friends. An initial gift in 1620 for the formation of a 'class library' in the humanities (classics and history) was followed by a further gift in 1646. Still maintained as a separate collection, it contains 64 volumes of continental works of the 16th and 17th centuries. This 'century of benefactions' was further enhanced in 1679 by Sir John Wedderburn (1599–1679), regent of St Leonard's College and physician to Charles I, who provided 136 volumes, including seven incunabula, and medical books of the 15th to 17th centuries. Towards the end of the 17th century the library was the site of important astronomical experiments carried out by James Gregory, Regius Professor of Mathematics, 1668–73. Using local landmarks, he established the position of a meridian line, which was later inlaid in the floor of the room.

In 1773 Samuel Johnson visited St Andrews and found it a thoroughly depressing experience. While

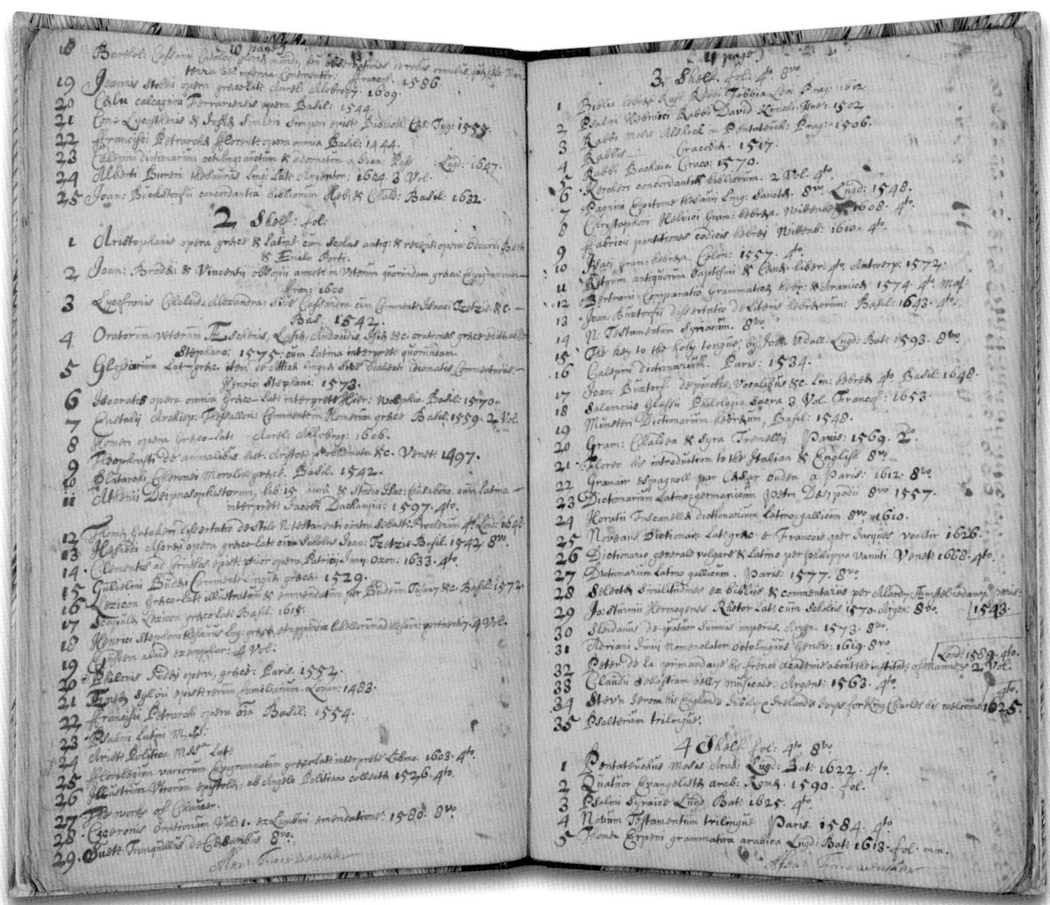

Press catalogue of the University Library, 1687. Each page is signed by the Librarian, Alexander Fairweather. UYLY105/2

acknowledging that he and Boswell were 'entertained with all the elegance of lettered hospitality', he described the city as a desolate wasteland. 'One of its streets is now lost; and in those that remain, there is the silence and solitude of inactive indigence and gloomy depopulation.' The dissolution of St Leonard's College (which in 1747 had been amalgamated with St Salvator's to form the United College of St Salvator and St Leonard) was a reproach to the nation. Its chapel was now pressed into service as a greenhouse, where even the plants failed to flourish. However, he found the university library 'not very spacious, but elegant and luminous' and recounted that 'the doctor, by whom it was shewn, hoped to irritate or subdue my English vanity by telling me, that we had no such repository of books in England'.

If the 18th century can be seen as a period of relative decline for the university as a whole, the story of the library in this period was a positive one, with considerable expansion of both book stock and premises. In common with the other British university libraries, the Copyright Act of 1709 gave St Andrews the right to claim a copy of every work published in Britain. Although far from everything was claimed, between 1710 and the loss of the copyright privilege in 1836 the steady flow of books from Stationers' Hall resulted in the strength of 18th-century collections being one of

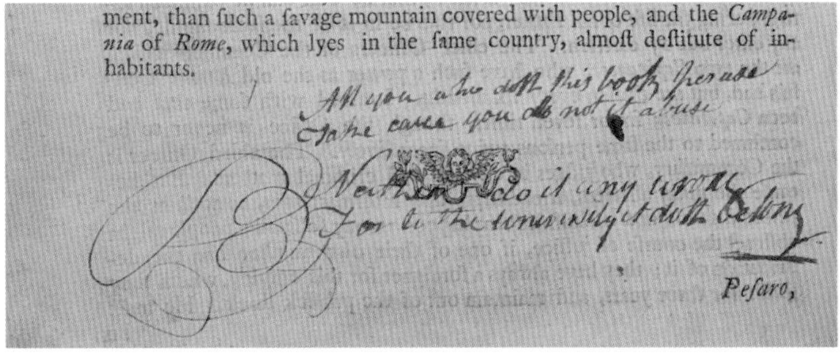

ment, than ſuch a ſavage mountain covered with people, and the *Campania* of *Rome*, which lyes in the ſame country, almoſt deſtitute of inhabitants.

All you who doth this book peruse
Take care you do not it abuse
Neither do it any wrong
For to the university it doth belong

Peſaro,

Many of the books from the copyright period are covered in scribbles and annotations by the students. Here readers are exhorted not to abuse the book. Other examples include remarks on the texts, scurrilous abuse of fellow students and staff, and a threat to murder the librarian one dark night. Joseph Addison, Works *Vol. 2 (London, 1721). s PR3300.D21*

Interior of the University Library, c.1898, by John Fairweather, contemporary with Margaret Oliphant's description. Note the 'curiosities' displayed in the foreground. GT-StAU-LibUp-001

Today this room is known as the King James Library.

the modern library's major assets. Of course, this led to a shortage of space, necessitating extensive remodelling of the library in 1764–7 (when the gallery was added). Further development occurred when the books from the old college libraries were transferred into the 'common' collection in 1783, and the collections continued to grow substantially throughout the 19th century, partially as a result of regular donations and bequests by university staff. Further extension and remodelling of the building was necessitated in the late 1820s (no. 7), and again, towards the south, in 1889–90, and in 1907 funded by the Carnegie Foundation.

Margaret Oliphant's atmospheric ghost story 'The Library Window' (*Blackwood's Magazine*, 1896) includes a 'conversation party' in the old College Library and briefly describes the interior of the room: 'The room was all light and bright, flowers wherever flowers could be, and the long lines of the books that went along the walls on each side, lighting up wherever there was a line of gilding or an ornament … On that side of the wall which was the street there seemed no windows at all. A long line of bookcases filled it from end to end.' Reference is also made to the 'curiosities' displayed in a glass case, including the original copy of the Solemn League and Covenant signed at St Andrews in 1643 and the Qur'an from the Library of Tipu Sultan (no. 48) and other items that still remain in the collections of the library or of the university museum.

Despite development of the collections and the buildings complex, the status of the library within the institution is perhaps best exemplified by the position of its librarian from 1881 to 1925, James Maitland Anderson. Also holding the offices of Secretary to the University, Quaestor, and Registrar and Secretary of the General Council, Anderson was an active historian of the university, publishing editions of some of its early records and several significant articles on its foundation and early history in association with the quincentenary celebrations held in 1911. It is hardly surprising that much of his time was taken up with other university business, with a consequent backlog in cataloguing and library management. Library opening hours – closed three mornings a week in winter, and open only six to eight hours a week in the summer – were a longstanding source of grievance for the students.

However, the collections – and the backlog – grew substantially through donations such as the libraries of Rev. Frederick Crombie, Professor of Divinity and Biblical Criticism (5,000 volumes, presented in 1890), and of Principal Sir James Donaldson (10,000 volumes, bequeathed in 1915). This tradition of benefaction continued throughout the 20th century, perhaps most strikingly with the gift by his son in 1929 of the remarkable library of avid book collector James David Forbes, principal of the United College from 1859 to 1868. His library includes some exceedingly rare scientific texts, now among the library's most prized possessions (nos. 5 and 37).

On 1 January 1925 George Herbert Bushnell took up office as University Librarian. According to his own notes, he was appointed to implement complete reorganization, recataloguing and classification of the library, 'as well as normal duties'. This was a formidable job description, but he tackled it with energy and determination. He found the books shelved by size wherever space was available, with no reference to subject. Bushnell enthusiastically introduced Library of Congress classification throughout the library, even attempting to apply it to the manuscripts, while for early printed books he devised a simple and elegant arrangement based on place and date of printing. The Upper Hall was riddled with woodworm and was structurally unsafe. Bushnell took a shelf to a Library Committee meeting and 'literally powdered it away on the table'. Major renovations were promptly carried out, copying the style of the old bookcases. This was when the position of Gregory's meridian line was inlaid into the new floorboards. Parliament Hall, then fully shelved, was cleared of bookcases for other purposes. In 'so-called spare moments' he compiled a *Library Manual*, published in 1926, which contains an invaluable record of decisions and procedures and makes fascinating reading today. All

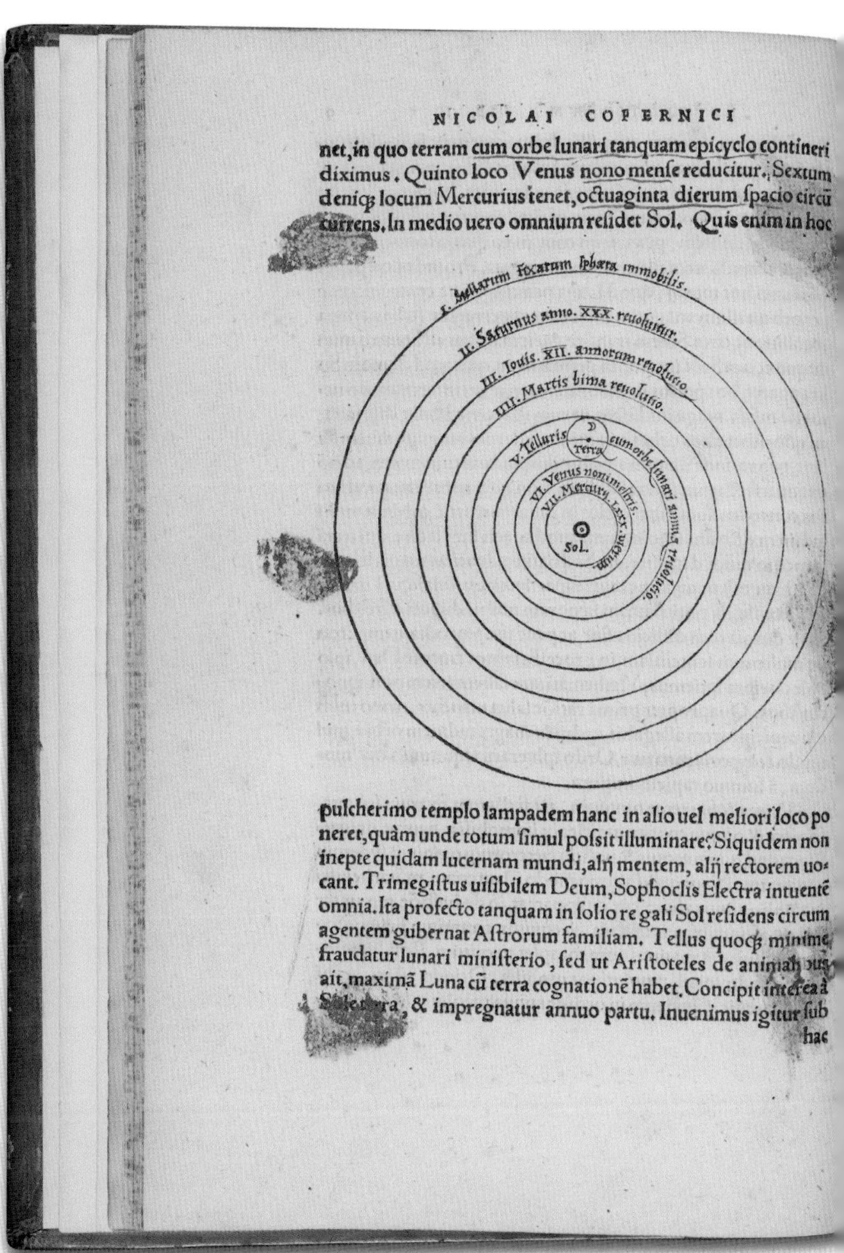

NICOLAI COPERNICI

net, in quo terram cum orbe lunari tanquam epicyclo contineri diximus. Quinto loco Venus nono mense reducitur. Sextum denique locum Mercurius tenet, octuaginta dierum spacio circũ currens. In medio uero omnium residet Sol. Quis enim in hoc

pulcherimo templo lampadem hanc in alio uel meliori loco poneret, quàm unde totum simul possit illuminare? Siquidem non inepte quidam lucernam mundi, alij mentem, alij rectorem uocant. Trimegistus uisibilem Deum, Sophoclis Electra intuentẽ omnia. Ita profecto tanquam in solio regali Sol residens circum agentem gubernat Astrorum familiam. Tellus quoque minime fraudatur lunari ministerio, sed ut Aristoteles de animali[illegible] ait, maximã Luna cũ terra cognationẽ habet. Concipit interea à [illegible]ra, & impregnatur annuo partu. Inuenimus igitur sub hac

Copernicus, De Revolutionibus *(Nuremberg, 1543), from the James David Forbes Collection. The wax stains may indicate that the controversial diagram showing the sun at the centre of the universe was obscured by an early owner. For QB41.C6B43*

The Arts and Divinity Reading Room in the late 19th-century extension. Photograph by George M. Cowie, 1965. StAU-SouS-Lib-62

George Herbert Bushnell on his last day in office, 17 March 1961. Photograph by George M. Cowie. GPS-GHB

library assistants, for example, were expected to study 'at least' Latin, Greek, French, German and English and were required to work towards the Library Association's examinations in librarianship.

Bushnell published widely on the history of the library, and his research notes are a valuable source of both information and speculation. His interest in their history led to the reassembling of many of the early donations of books, which had been dispersed throughout the library, into named 'special collections', and it was during his time in office that systematic work on the manuscripts began, anticipating the formation of a dedicated manuscripts department in 1959.

By 1970 the existing library complex was hopelessly overcrowded, and the university began to look seriously at building a new library on a different but still central site. The purchase of St Katharine's School, lying between North Street and the Scores, created an opportunity to locate the new library within the historic city, adjacent to the United College. The site presented challenges, however, principally because planning regulations restricted the height of the new building in relation to the iconic spire of St Salvator's Chapel. The architects Faulkner-Brown Hendy Watkinson Stonor, whose design for Nottingham University Library in the 1960s had won them several other academic library contracts, accordingly presented a phased design, intended to be extended to the north in two stages as rising student numbers demanded. Site work began in August 1972, and, after transferring stock, staff and services from South Street, Phase 1 of the new library opened to readers in August 1976. The historic 17th-century building in South Street was retained as a library for divinity, mediaeval history and psychology.

The current building is on four floors, with the lowest, Level 1, partially underground due to the north–south slope of the site. In accordance with Harry Faulkner-Brown's influential principles of library design, the interior was flexible and mainly open-plan, incorporating the latest developments in environmental control into a

The current Main Library building under construction, 1974 (anon.). StAu-NorS-Lib-109

low-maintenance layout. The exterior, with concrete shelves projecting at each level beyond the walls of brown and bronze-tinted glass, was described by John Gifford in his architectural guide to Fife as 'almost but not quite elegant'.

Phases 2 and 3 of the original design were never built. After 30 years, with a huge increase in student numbers and a revolution in information technology, the Director of Library Services declared the building unable to cope with the learning and research needs of the 21st-century university. Planning is currently underway for a renovation of the main library building as the first phase of a longer term commitment to significant investment in the library's facilities, services and collections. As the university approaches its 600th anniversary, here is an opportunity to demonstrate that it is not just the venerable history of St Andrews University Library that is worth celebrating, but its vibrant future too.

Elizabeth Henderson

St Andrews University Library, 2007. Photograph by Rhona Rutherford.

Spotlight on the Special Collections

The Special Collections Department, as well as being responsible for a wide range of academic and outreach activities, has as its primary role the preservation and provision of access (for both the university and broader communities) to four main collections.

The Rare Books

Libraries differ in their definitions of what constitutes a 'rare' book. At St Andrews everything printed before 1861 is treated as a rare book, as are especially scarce or valuable later items, such as first editions of Virginia Woolf or private press publications. Entire libraries or collections are generally kept together under the name of the collector and range in scope from the tightly focused (the Williams Collection of editions of the *Eikon Basilike*) to the cheerfully diverse (the Beveridge Collection of books about Norway, Esperanto and beekeeping). We continue to purchase carefully selected items to support the teaching and research of the university, and examples of recent purchases are included in this book.

Theology, philosophy of religion and church history are particularly well represented, through the substantial libraries of Baron Friedrich von Hügel (1852–1925), episcopal minister and liturgiologist George Hay Forbes (1821–75) and others. The strength of the history of science holdings is due both to the superb J.D. Forbes Collection and also to the university's active acquisition of key scientific works since the 17th century. The outstanding library of scholar and antiquary David Hay Fleming (1849–1931), consisting of over 13,000 volumes, manuscripts and photographs, was bequeathed to the town and people of St Andrews and has been in the safekeeping of the University Library since 2000, a goldmine for local history research.

We encourage the use of rare books for teaching, and increasing numbers of students of subjects from mediaeval literature to biology have the opportunity to work closely with original material.

Elizabeth Henderson

The Manuscripts

The manuscripts section contains a wonderfully eclectic mix of material, from mediaeval to modern. Although a separate Manuscripts Department was not established until 1959, manuscripts have been coming into the custody of the university for centuries, a few tracing back to the mediaeval libraries of St Andrews. Because of the lack, until recently, of a local authority archive in Fife, the library was the natural home for records of the local history of St Andrews and northeast Fife. There are church and burgh records, estate records, architectural plans, business records, solicitors' deeds fetched in packing cases and out of attics, as well as the personal and working records of many university staff. Holdings continue to grow by gift, bequest and purchase. In a wider context, deposits include letters and diaries by the Catholic Modernists, literary papers and an intriguing Asian collection.

These provide a rich resource for researchers both at home and abroad, including local historians, genealogists and house history hunters, as well as for a wide range of academic projects. Documents are provided for lecturers holding classes in English, history and divinity, and indeed across the university. Others are used by the department for teaching palaeography, manuscript handling and use, and in providing items for exhibition. From books of hours, sermons of an itinerant preacher, an Esperanto order of service, notes on séances, letters home from early Scottish settlers in Canada, America and Australia, an album of pressed flowers, a grammar book for the West African Fula language, a beautiful lacquer-covered Qur'an, the collection holds many fascinating items – and many surprises.

Maia Sheridan

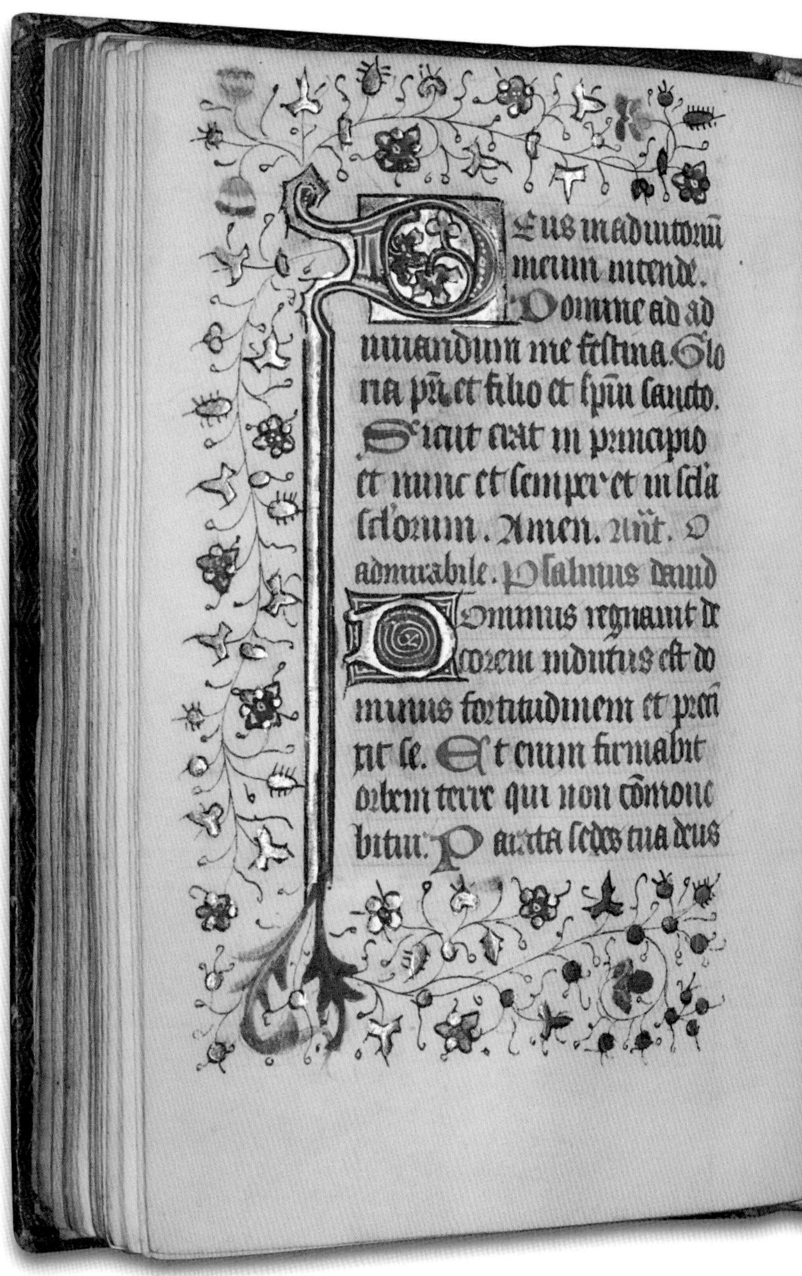

Illuminated page from a Book of Hours, open at the beginning of Lauds from the Hours of the Virgin, with the start of Psalm 93 (France, c.1450). msBX2080.F6

The Muniments

The institutional archive embodies the corporate memory of the University of St Andrews. These official records relate to its properties, management, students and teaching and begin in 1215, predating the foundation of the university, since the property acquired by the university and its colleges has an earlier recorded history. Hugely varied in form and content, of particular significance are the core mediaeval records, the 16th- to 19th-century college diet books, the inventoried papers and titles of the colleges, the library archive and records of student societies from 1760 onwards. The collection continues to grow as modern material in both traditional and digital formats, important as historical record, falls out of current administrative use.

As well as for regular genealogical and biographical enquiry, and the frequent investigation of issues in relation to current institutional business, the muniments are widely used for research into a vast range of local, national and international topics and as sources for teaching. They have been heavily mined in the course of the ongoing History of the Universities Project, many of whose staff and students have contributed to this volume. The story of the university's 600 years is preserved within the historic records. Recent and current efforts to improve their cataloguing and to promote their wealth as a research resource ensure that they remain central to the university's life and play a full part in events such as the forthcoming sexcentenary celebrations.

Rachel Hart

Universitati Academicae Sancti Andreae
Praeses Sociique Regii Medicorum Collegii Edinburgensis
Salutem plurimam dicimus.

Liceat nobis, viri praestantissimi, venerabili Academiae Sancti Andreae, natalicia sacra post quingentos annos feliciter redeuntia celebraturae, admirationem nostram et gratulationem testificari. Jure equidem occasione tam fausta laetamini, nosque, recordantes quanta benificia patriae per tot saecula contuleritis, ex toto animo caerimoniis gaudiisque vestris intersumus.

Altrix enim litterarum atque omnium artium bonarum prima in Caledonia extitit vestra Academia, neque unquam eam, ex quo constitua est, vires defecerant; immo vero et pro temporum vicissitudine semper quantum valeret demonstravit et nunc quantum valeat demonstrat. Quod sane cultioribus, sive Scotorum sive peregrinorum, omnibus pergratum est; quotquot enim doctrinam ex animo persequuntur sese communi veritatis amore scientiaeque studio sentiant esse conexos. Nos autem vincula artiora cum vobis coniungunt, namque ex huius Collegii Sociis multos eximiosque numerare possemus qui alumni vestrae Academiae fuerunt, et multis in rerum discriminibus vestram erga nos benevolentiam experti sumus.

Itaque pro perenni rerum vestrarum incolumitate et prosperitate pia et sincera vota nuncupamus, optantes ut fortuna vestra ad communem patriae utilitatem semper capiat incrementa.

Valete et nobis, sicut favetis, favetote.

Byrom Bramwell Praeses.
Harry Rainy Secretarius.

Illuminated address presented to the University of St Andrews on the occasion of the celebration of its quincentenary by the Royal College of Physicians of Edinburgh, September 1911. UYUY185/E/1

The Photographs

In 1839 a close friendship between two great scientists, the British inventor of photography and the principal of the United College at St Andrews, was the genesis of what is now known as the St Andrews University Library Photographic Collection. It was in St Andrews that the earliest practitioners of photography in Scotland would hone their skills and master this new science and art, taking influential first steps and pioneering notions of the medium's potential. In the 1970s the University Library began formally collecting photography, establishing its historical, educational, and artistic importance within the university and to the greater public. With momentum building, successions of vast photographic acquisitions would add rare and unique images from across the British Isles. Through a marriage of several generations of seminal photographers as well as previously hidden luminaries, we now present a world-class collection to an international audience for both academic and personal research. It provides an extensive cross-disciplinary primary resource, documenting the socio-cultural transformation of Scotland and beyond from the 1840s onward.

Since the 1990s, striving to bring history to bear on the present through digitization and the online presentation of historic photography, we have extended the collection's audience far beyond its immediate community. Now internationally recognized, photography's rich and influential role in social, cultural, historic and artistic development is made manifest and increasingly accessible through new and engaging technologies.

Marc Boulay

Miss J. N. *Photograph by Alexander Wilson Hill,* c.*1904–40. Bromoil Transfer Print. AWH-83*

The Treasures

Bible, *Latin Vulgate (Rouen, 1511). Said to be the foundation bible of St Leonard's College, there are copious annotations round the text and the names of several students on the inside back board. The signature of Robert Wilkie, principal of St Leonard's College 1589–1611, and the date 1604 are just visible on the front paste down. Bound in calf over oak boards, there is a worn panel stamp of the Crucifixion on the upper board. A chain remains attached to the lower edge of the front board. It is possible that this book was bound in the Augustinian Priory of St Andrews. Bib BS75.B11*

Vniuersis sancte matris ecclesie filiis. Walterus dei gratia prior de sancto Andrea. et Con-
uentus eiusdem loci salutem. Sciatis omnes tam futuri quam presentes. nos dedisse
et Concessisse et hac nostra carta confirmasse Hugoni pincerne et heredibus suis terram
nostram quam emimus a magistro Malpodoco. primam videlicet terre illi que fuit quondam
Cuthberti decani a parte orientali. Tenendam sibi et heredibus suis libere et quiete
ab omni seruicio et exactione et Consuetudine. Reddendo nobis inde annuatim tres
solidos. dimidium ad pascha et dimidium ad festum sancti Michaelis. Testibus his.
Willelmo Capello de Bucssyn. Radulfo et Iohanne clericis domini [illegible]. Germano. Roberto
de Rokesbord. Magistro Radulfo. Alexandro fridegend. [illegible] burgensibus sancti An-
Iohanne de Bereforda. Willelmo de Ardit. Et aliis quam pluribus.

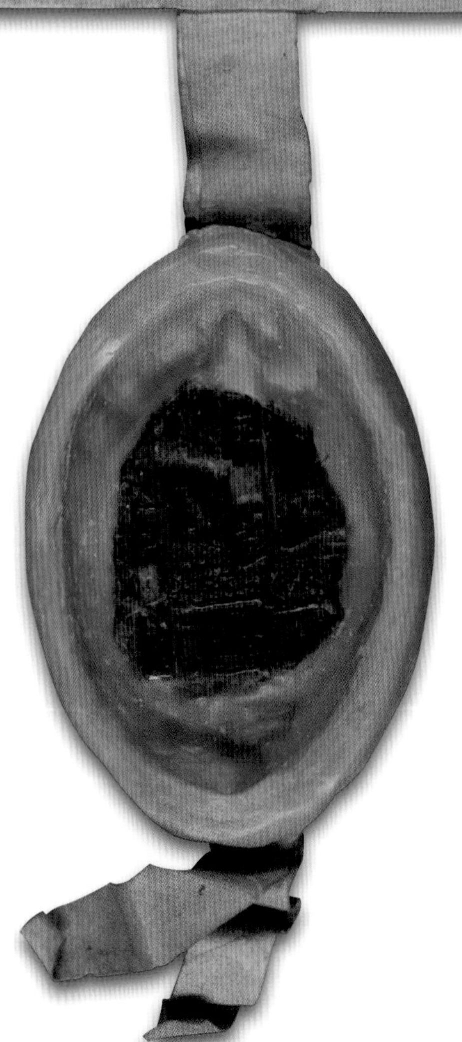

1 12th-century St Andrews: A Cultural Mix

Charter of Walter, prior of St Andrews, 1189–95

Parchment, 117 × 173mm plus single tag bearing repaired pendant seal
Provenance: held with muniments from unknown date; transferred to manuscript collection, 1965
ms30276

The writing of a charter, a single sheet of parchment with a text usually in Latin and with a wax seal, was the standard way of recording a grant of property or rights in the Middle Ages. This is an example, written in typical late 12th-century Scottish documentary handwriting, in which the prior and convent of St Andrews convey land for an annual rent to Hugh Pincerna, that is, 'Butler'. At this period the name is almost certainly not his surname but a description of his office: he is the man in charge of a lord's drink (an honourable position). Since Hugh Pincerna occurs frequently in the charters of the bishops of St Andrews, he is likely to have been the bishop's butler. The land is identified as that which the priory had purchased from Master Malpatrick and its location given as adjacent on the eastern side to the land that had belonged to Dean Cuthbert. It is not usual for such documents to bear a date at this time, but it is possible to infer that this charter was issued in the years 1189–95 by the mentions of Prior Walter (1160–95) and two 'clergy of the bishop-elect'. The bishop-elect is Roger, son of the earl of Leicester, who was appointed bishop of St Andrews in 1189 but, for unknown reasons, not consecrated until 1198. The rent of three shillings a year was payable in two instalments, at Easter and Michaelmas (29 September), a common pair of rent-terms. At this period the shilling was not a coin but a unit of account, representing 12 silver pennies.

The personal names in the charter are an interesting mixture. Master Malpatrick bears a Gaelic name (meaning 'serf of Patrick'), Dean Cuthbert has the same name as the great Anglo-Saxon saint, while the prior and several of the witnesses bear the Anglo-Norman names that had become common after the Norman conquest of England in 1066. This cultural mix is also reflected in the appearance among the witnesses of Alexander the Frenchman, a burgess of St Andrews.

The seal was attached as a way of authenticating a document in the age before signatures developed that function. The example here is fragmentary, but complete examples of the seal of St Andrews Priory are known from other documents. As was generally the case with ecclesiastical seals, the shape is oval, like women's seals, but unlike the round seals of laymen. The image apparently depicts the cathedral, although there is doubt regarding how detailed and realistic a representation was intended. The complete examples contain the words 'the seal of the church of St Andrew the Apostle in Scotland', in Latin, around the edge. One of the two crosses shown above the church is a saltire, which raises the interesting possibility that this symbol was already associated with St Andrew and Scotland. In the following century the priory did have a seal depicting the saint crucified on an X-shaped cross, as in mediaeval legend, but the seal depicted here is earlier and may, indeed, be the earliest surviving example of the famous symbol.

Robert Bartlett

2 Documenting Nostalgia

George Allan Little, 'Boatbuilding at Anstruther', 1973

Gelatin silver print, 200 × 258mm
Provenance: from the G.A. Little Collection, gift of the Little family, 2000
GAL-22

Allan Little (1919–98) left his career as a banker in Dundee in 1966 to pursue his calling as a photographer. Working freelance, he was obliged to take on many different types of photographic commissions, such as documenting events, conducting portrait sittings and photographing for schools. However, more than anything, Allan Little's newly adopted trade was spurred on by a desire for change in his life and a profound interest in the people he would encounter and in the stories that surrounded their lives. Through the application of patient observation, his camera's lens and his writing, he would devote the next 20 years to the exploration and expression of local and regional cultures, their respective histories and the people who were the product of the urban and rural environments surrounding Dundee, Fife and the northeast of Scotland. Of a conservative and traditional temperament, Little's editorial photography speaks of an affection for traditional crafts, trades and artisans and the fortitude of spirit and cultural tenacity required to maintain such ways of life along Scotland's east coast.

Distinct from the spontaneity of daily photo-journalism, Little carefully researched and actively proposed photographic essays and articles to well-recognized editorial magazines. These included publications such as *Scottish Field*, *The Scots Magazine* and *The Lady*, each catering to an established demographic – ardent consumers of tourism with strong interests in history. Through these publishers he found a voice and an audience for narratives that illustrated cultural practices as well as grand and traditional architecture, all couched within a framework self-consciously appreciative of the way things once were.

Little's approach to his subjects was non-invasive. Rather, his practice was to establish relationships with his subjects, put them at ease and represent them in a manner that would speak honestly of their person, while highlighting the significance of their community or trade. His photographically illustrated articles at once celebrated the individuality, character and values of Scotland's past, yet also conformed these to the sensibilities of a middle- and upper-class readership who had a particular view of the history and traditions of their country.

Taking into account his intent as a photographer, the photographic content of his work and the way in which different audiences were exposed to it, Allan Little's images illustrate how important it is that photography be interpreted from multiple perspectives. The meaning of a photograph is fluid: it has the ability to change throughout its life, from the initial moment of creative inspiration, to the instant a frame is placed around a scene both to include and to exclude information. Symptomatic of an inherently reproducible medium, the manner in which photographs are juxtaposed, the contexts of their initial presentation or later appropriation and reuse and the perspective of their various audiences over time, all serve to change and add complexity to their meaning.

The University Library's Photographic Collection holds over 560 individual photographs by Allan Little, and these stand as homage to honest labour, traditional trades and regional culture. To appreciate these works fully, however, it is necessary to acknowledge that, while Little's editorial photographic work is a sincere interpretation of his subjects, at the same time it cannot be divorced from the demands and attitudes of the social classes that funded and would consume it. Through the commercialization and nostalgic visual stylization of Scottish history and culture, that which is foreign as a result of distance, time or class is transformed into a tool of empowerment and distinction, affirming the readers' values and socio-cultural attitudes and yet having an equal impact on the subjects photographed. It is the discord between the multiple interpretations of a given photograph that gives the medium its richness as an historical record.

Marc Boulay

3 Golden-age Tales of a Small Land

The Original Chronicle of Andrew Wyntoun, *c.*1550

Paper, 245 × 175mm, in modern binding
Provenance: appears in library catalogue, 1810
msDA775.A6W9

In the late Middle Ages Scotland witnessed a golden age of historical writing. Chronicles and verses were produced that shaped the way that Scots understood their place in the world, and *The Original Chronicle* was one of the most popular of these works. Composed in the second decade of the 15th century, this history wove together biblical and classical episodes to form a narrative into which myths about the Scots' own origins could be fitted. From these stories the chronicle moved on to recent centuries, focusing on Scotland's kings and conflicts. *The Original Chronicle* was one of the most copied works in 15th- and 16th-century Scotland, and both the chronicle itself and this manuscript of it have strong links to St Andrews. The work's author was Andrew Wyntoun (*c.*1350–*c.*1422), a cleric who had been one of the canons of St Andrews Cathedral. When he wrote his work, Wyntoun was head of the priory of St Serf on an island in Loch Leven some 20 miles west of St Andrews, and his chronicle is peppered with details of the surrounding area.

Wyntoun wrote with a local audience in mind, and a Fife baron, Sir John Wemyss, was his patron. While the manuscript held in St Andrews (one of only nine surviving manuscripts of the text) was copied nearly 150 years later, its production shows that the work still appealed to laymen. An inscription in the text records that to 'Patrik of Lermontht of Dersy knyt this bouk pertines of ryt' (i.e., was owned by him). Lermonth was both laird of Dairsie and a burgess of St Andrews, and he was the town's provost in 1555 and had close links to the royal court. It was the class of literate lesser nobles that looked to Wyntoun for knowledge of their country's past. This popularity was because *The Original Chronicle* was the first history of Scotland written in the tongue Wyntoun terms 'inglis', rather than the usual scholarly language, Latin. In choosing 'oure langage', Wyntoun deliberately served his lay audience. The St Andrews copy of the work was no decorative object of status but a practical text, dotted with notations, showing its use by early readers.

Though Wyntoun's efforts to relay history in rhyming couplets rather than in prose perhaps detracts from the seriousness of the work, *The Original Chronicle* contributed to the way Scotland's past was written. Two of the key figures in this history, Macbeth and William Wallace, emerge, for the first time, in their lasting characters. Wyntoun's Macbeth is haunted by the prophecies of 'thre werd systeris' who foretell his rise and fall, while Wallace is driven to avenge the taunts of English soldiers and the killing of his wife.

Wyntoun was not simply a storyteller. His account of events from the 1330s to 1408 is one of the key sources for this lively period of Scotland's history. It confirms Andrew Wyntoun as one of the group of Scottish writers who was keen to examine a world in which classical and biblical authorities sat alongside the tales of their own small land.

Michael Brown

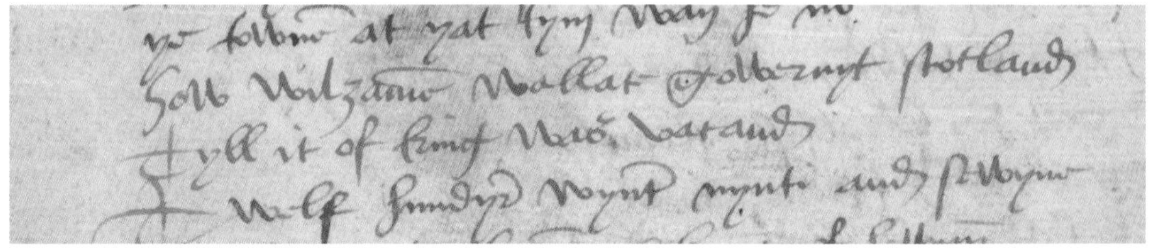

Agane yt lorde myt prensit be
hys systor sone yat he luffit weile
wt a slycht tuke hys castell
And ye ȝoung erle of douglass
Throw hym yan in entryt was
Bot all yis he excusit weile
As I befor said ilka deile
The gude duke of albany
Witnessit his stait lettirly
Na mair befor consentit he
yat yt gude lorde suld spulit be
hys part yarfor and his payne
he did to bring yt lorde agane
Now eftyr Sr Waltyr traylleis deiss
Quha to yat stait promowit was
A thowsande four hundyr ȝeir and ane
ffra Ihu Cst had manhede tane
ye bisshope of sanct androwis se
A lorde commendyt of bewte
To all wertewis apperande
Godlykly his lyff ledande
Wele and wyss in all consaile
And cunnande in all gouernale
A solempne clerk be grais
Rolowyt be syndry faculteis
In alkyn dede war and wyss
And yt devot in hys serwys
Mast Waltyr trayle be nayme
yis lordy of commendyt fame
hys saule ȝauld tyll his creatur
hys body tyll hallowyt sepultur
The kyrke of scotland mycht sair
ye tynsall of yat gude pyllar
Quhen yis gude lorde wt honour

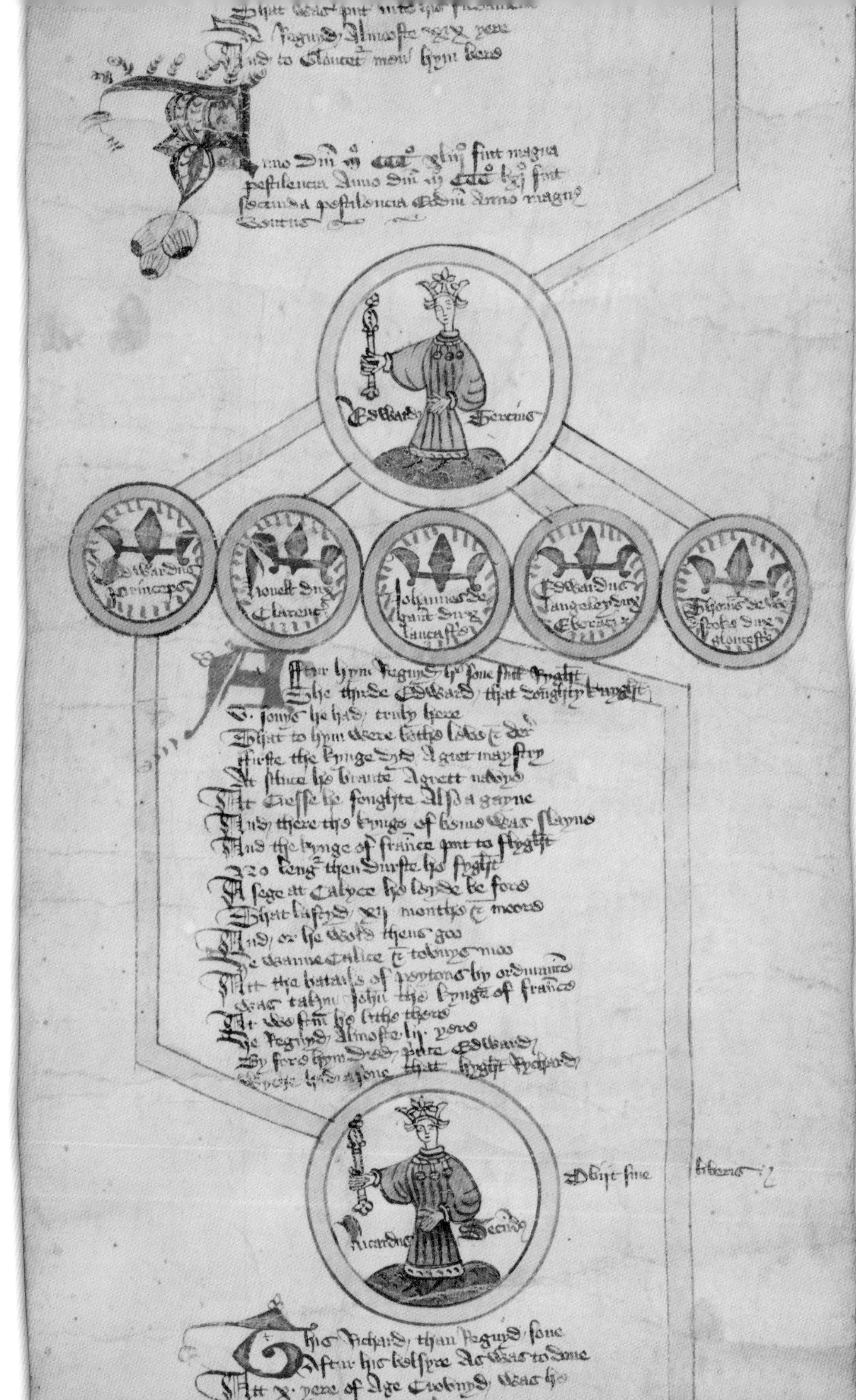

That was put into the [illegible]
He regned almoste xx yere
And to Glaucett men hym bere

Anno domini m° ccc° xlix° fuit magna
pestilencia. Anno domini m° ccc° lxi fuit
secunda pestilencia. Anno domini magnus
ventus

After hym regned his sone that hyght
The thryde Edward that doughty knyght
v. sonys he had truly here
That to hym were bothe lefe and dere
Furste the kynge dyd a gret maystry
At Sluce his brante a grett navye
At Cresse he foughte also agayne
And there the kynge of Beme was slayne
And the kynge of France went to flyght
No lenger then durste he fyght
A sege at Calyce he layde be fore
That lasted xii monthis and more
And or he wold thens goo
He wanne Calice and townys moo
At the batails of Poytours by ordynaunce
Was takyn John the kynge of France
It was [illegible] his lyffe there
He regned almoste lii yere
By fore hym dyed prince Edward
[illegible] sone that hyght Rychard

This Richard than regned sone
After his belsyre as was to done
At x yere of age crowned was he

4 England's Supremacy in Royal Propaganda

Genealogical roll of the kings of England, 15th century

Parchment, 1,924 × 195mm
Provenance: gift of anonymous donor, 2003
ms38660

Among royal propaganda produced in the reign of Henry VI were verse chronicles of the English kings outlining their succession since William the Conqueror. The best-known such poem was written by John Lydgate, but there were also anonymous versions, and the St Andrews example is one of these. Such reminders of English history were a means of providing reassurance during the minority of Henry VI, and were also used to justify the legitimacy of the Lancastrian regime. The unbroken line of royal succession is visually emphasized by the illustrated genealogy that accompanies the verses in many of the surviving copies. Representations of the kings are presented within centrally placed medallions, from which lines of descent are marked to show how the crown passed from father to son or to another close male relative.

Each king is depicted as a crowned figure holding a sceptre, standing on a green mound; the full-length portraits are identical and unremarkable. Beneath each medallion are lines of English verse set in rhyming couplets; at various points there are also Latin prose notes that give more historical details. The amount of verse allocated to each king varies: Stephen and Richard I receive only ten lines each, but Edward III is given 20 lines, and John 22.

Certain types of information are common to each entry. Each stanza begins by introducing the king and his right to succeed and concludes by noting the number of years of his reign and his place of burial. In between, some of the significant events or achievements in the reign of each monarch are mentioned. In the example given here, showing the stanza relating to Edward III, the events referred to are: Edward's destruction of the French navy at Sluys in 1340; the Battle of Crécy in 1346 when John, King of Bohemia was killed and Philip VI of France was routed; the successful siege of Calais in 1347, which lasted almost a year; and the Battle of Poitiers in 1356 at which John II of France was captured. All collectively demonstrate England's supremacy over its near neighbour, a relevant issue in the 1430s and 1440s when the English were struggling to protect their interests in France.

The St Andrews copy, like several others, is in the form of a roll rather than a manuscript book. Unfortunately, it is now incomplete: the third membrane of the roll is missing, and the verses after the section relating to Richard II are lost. The advantage of the roll format was that it was extremely portable and might easily be displayed for public instruction – the St Andrews copy does, in fact, show signs of having been nailed up in this way.

An inscription, now damaged and partly lost, at the head of the roll shows that it was owned by William Cayton, who in the 1470s was the prior of Watton, a house of the Gilbertine order near to Beverley in Yorkshire.

Margaret Connolly

5 Perfectly Proportioned

Luca Pacioli, *Divina Proportione*, 1509

Venice: Alessandro and Paganino de Paganini, 1509
4to, 281 × 198mm
Provenance: from the library of James David Forbes, presented by George Forbes, 1929

Luca Pacioli (*c.*1445–1517), also known as Luca di Borgo after his birthplace at Borgo San Sepolcro in Tuscany, was a Franciscan friar. He travelled widely in Italy and beyond, living in most of the major Italian cities as well as in Zara (Zadar in modern Croatia). He taught mathematics privately and in several universities. His three published works are *Summa de Arithmetica, Geometria, Proportioni e Proportionalita* (1494), *Divina Proportione* (1509) and an edition of Euclid's *Elements of Geometry* (1509). All were published in Venice by the same printers. Copies of all three texts are contained in the outstanding scientific library of James David Forbes, principal of the United College at the University of St Andrews from 1859 to 1868.

The *Summa* was a popular but unoriginal compilation, noted for its accounts of an early form of algebra and of mercantile arithmetic and for the first published description of double-entry bookkeeping. The St Andrews copy is the second edition of 1523, published in Toscolano. The *Elements* was a reissue of the 1482 Latin edition by Campanus, with emendations and notes by Pacioli. The St Andrews copy of the *Elements* is bound with the *Divina Proportione*. All three works are beautifully printed, with ornate titles and woodcut capital letters and diagrams. Some other unpublished works by Pacioli survive elsewhere in manuscript, including a treatise on chess.

The *Divina Proportione*, here illustrated, was partly written in Milan during 1496–7. Like the *Summa*, it is in Italian rather than Latin. The first of its three parts concerns Euclid's 'division in extreme and mean ratio' – Pacioli's divine proportion – followed by descriptions of regular and semi-regular polyhedral solids. The second part concerns architecture, based largely on Vitruvius, and also describes the ideal proportions of Roman lettering. The third part is an Italian translation of a Latin work by Piero della Francesca on regular solids.

The 'division in extreme and mean ratio' is easily explained. Consider a straight line AB and locate the point C on the line between A and B such that the ratio of the length AB to the length AC is the same as the ratio of the length AC to the length CB. In other words, $(a + b) : b = b : a$. These ratios turn out to equal $(1 + \sqrt{5})/2$, later dubbed the 'golden ratio'. Though Pacioli praises its 'inestimable' mathematical properties, the mathematical content of the work is slight. His main aim is to expound the ratio's aesthetic merits for use in art and architecture. In recent times, 'golden numberism' has acquired mystical significance, erroneously thought to underlie the proportions of many famous buildings and works of art.

In his youth, Pacioli probably studied under Piero della Francesca, whose studio was in San Sepolcro. Pacioli was also a close friend of Leonardo da Vinci, and the many excellent full-page diagrams of regular and semi-regular solids in *Divina Proportione* are believed to be Leonardo's work. Few mathematicians can have had a more talented illustrator for their book.

Alex D.D. Craik

Dodecaedron Apotetmimenon Epirmenon Cenon

Dodecaedron Abſciſum Eleuatum Vacuum

6 A 'Most Scandalous Book'

Library receipt books and borrowing registers, 1737–1925

46 manuscript volumes, various sizes
Provenance: working record of the library
UYLY205 – UYLY209

The most scandalous book ever written in St Andrews is Robert Chambers's *Vestiges of the Natural History of Creation*. Claiming to be 'the first attempt to connect the natural sciences into a history of creation', it was published in October 1844 and convulsed Victorian intellectual life. Charles Darwin read Chambers's work with fascination, and it helped shape his thinking. Other excited readers ranged from Queen Victoria to Abraham Lincoln, from George Eliot and Florence Nightingale to Arthur Schopenhauer and Ralph Waldo Emerson. Radical thinkers devoured the book, which explained how creation 'evolved'.

Chambers, co-founder with his brother William of the famous Chambers publishing house, lived in St Andrews with his family at Abbey Park in the early 1840s. *Vestiges* was published anonymously. In St Andrews only Robert's wife, Anne, who copied out his original manuscript in her own hand, knew who had written it. He was described by his daughter as having written *Vestiges* in St Andrews 'with all the security of a criminal unrecognized in the midst of the police'. He mixed with the university principal and professors but kept much of his work secret. It has been assumed that he relied on his private library to fuel his scandalous book. However, the remarkably well-preserved borrowing records of the University of St Andrews Library show that he made intense use of that library while he wrote *Vestiges*, borrowing a range of books from popular encyclopedias to the work of pioneering geologists, such as Henry De La Beche.

The library archive is extensive and includes reader registration material from 1697 with borrowing records from 1737–59 and 1768–1925. There are lists of books scattered throughout the muniment collection, but the fine series of catalogues begins in 1644 and, thanks to the library's legal deposit status, there are records of Stationers' Hall books from 1710 to 1837. Librarians' correspondence from 1850 and acquisition and financial records amplify the evidence of the historic workings of the library.

While the borrowing registers give a unique insight into the way one of the 19th-century's most shocking books was nourished, more generally they let us see what many hundreds of 18th- and 19th-century students, professors and others (almost all male) wanted to read. Some book-borrowers are famous St Andrews alumni, from James Wilson, one of the signatories of the American Declaration of Independence, to Robert Burns's future landlord and friend Robert Riddell. Others are long forgotten. Yet the fullness and detail of the borrowing registers also allow historians and critics to track general patterns of reading. So, for instance, we can see how, when St Andrews in the mid-18th century became one of the world's first universities to teach English-language literary texts, the teenage boy students were eager consumers of novels. They particularly liked novels about women's lives with titles like *The Female Spy*. Modern scholars have begun to interpret the significance of what earlier generations of students were reading, but the borrowing registers remain a largely untapped and unusual resource: one of the hidden treasures of St Andrews University Library.

Robert Crawford

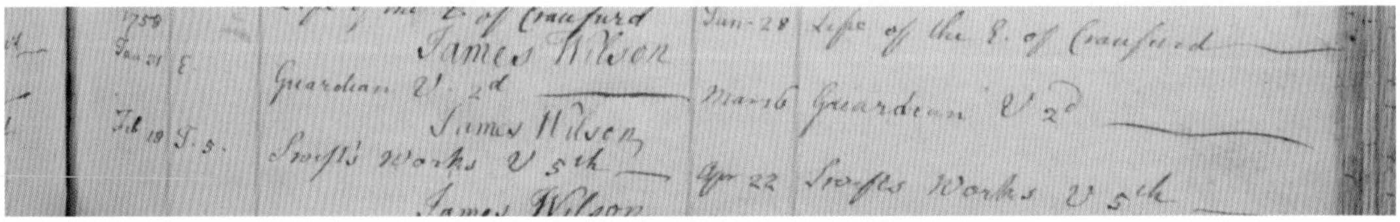

Mr Chambers

22. A 3 4 11 Bracebridge Hall 1.2
A D 6 35 Sketch book
Gentleman Magazine 60, 61, 62, 62, 63, 63, 70
Ency Edinb Philosophical Trans 2
J J 3.1 Philo Trans. 16
C 1216 Ben Johnson x.2.3.4.5.6.7.8.9
C 8 Beaumont Fletcher 1.2.3.4.5 6.7.8.9.11
A H 5 17 Webster 1.2.3.4
E H 22 Marmion
Blackwood Mg. XX.X.X
Edinb Phil. Journal 26 27
B 8 Merchiston Silurian
B 2 1 4 McCulloch 1.2.3
B D 1 3 8 Sections
B P 2 16 De la Beche
Trans Geo. Soc 3
A I 2.9 Brown
R E 5.3 Parkinson 1.2.3
B P 2 16 De la Beche
A H Opium eater
B 2 7 64 Idler Mag 1.2.3
B 2 Rafles Jewish Antiquities 1.2
A H 2 30 Evelyn 1.2
C 11 8 Fuller 1.2
Jameson Phil Journal 22
C K 7 9 Napier
B D 4 7 Burnet 2
J M Metropolis 1.2
Pinnock guide 1
Penny Magazine 16
Philosophical Journal Oct
Philosophical Transactions 48.49, 50, 51.52
C L 1 3 7 Philosophy Health 1.2
Lardner Electricity
Cycl. Anatomy pt 20
B K 2 16 Dunbery
C J 13 9 Carpenter
E F 4 9 Crabbe 1.2.3

7 The Historic Heart of the University

Architectural drawing of the University Library by Robert Reid, 1827

Paper, 324 × 543mm
Provenance: presented by the Ministry of Works, Edinburgh, *c.*1952
UYUY1381/18b/3

This architectural drawing of South Street Library and part of St Mary's College shows a building of immense historic significance, constructed on a site that has been in the ownership of the university since St John's College was established there in 1419. This is one of a collection of historic drawings of university buildings

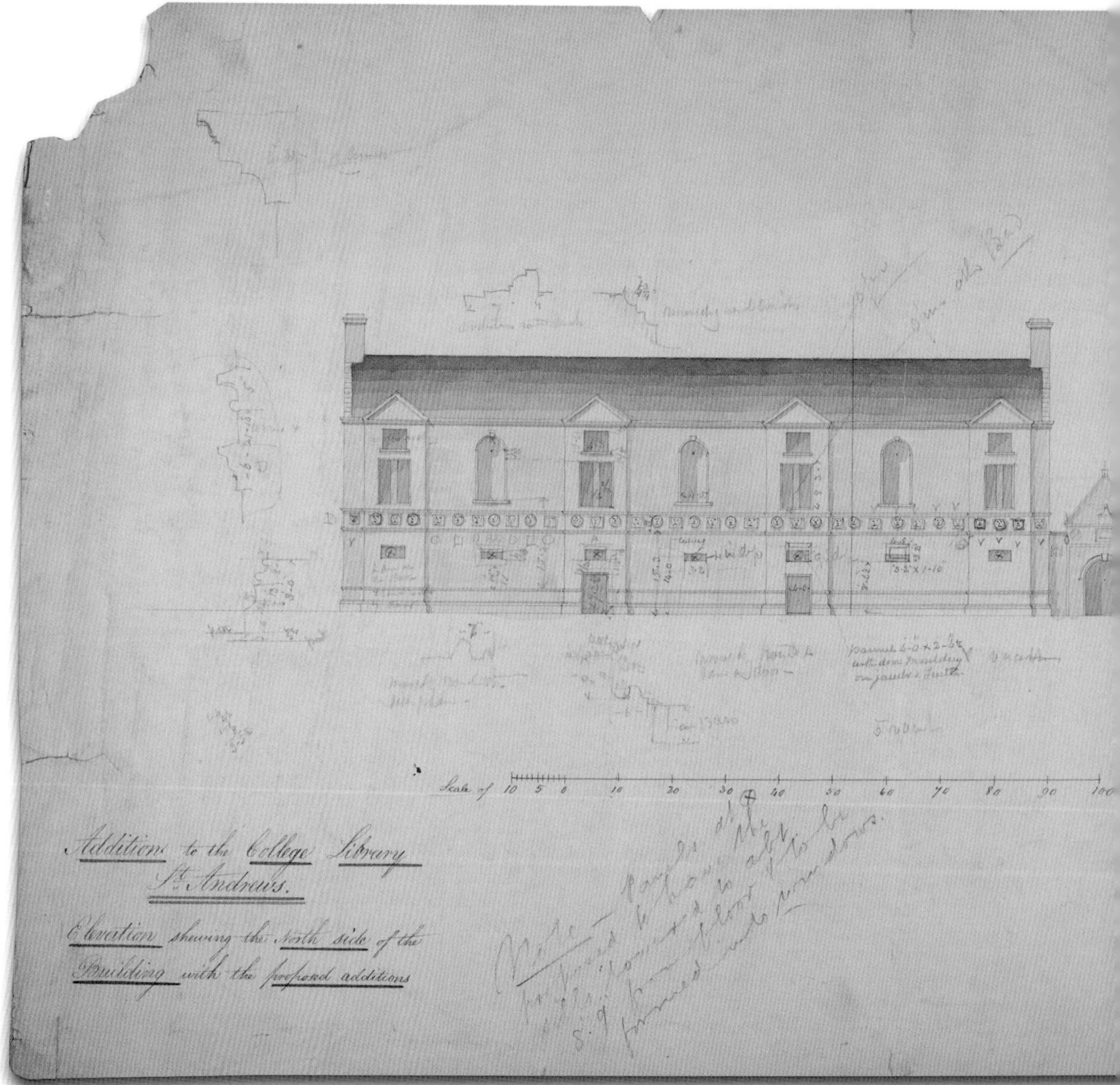

that, in conjunction with other material, including the archive of the St Andrews architectural practice of James Gillespie and Scott and the surviving drawings of the St Andrews Dean of Guild Court, make a major contribution to the understanding of the architectural development of the university and town.

The working drawing of the 'Addition to the College Library' presents a building that appears to be of a single date but that, in reality, with the proposed addition, would be one of several distinct periods. The core of the five bays to the left is likely to incorporate some of the fabric of the 15th-century pedagogy, although this part of the structure largely dates from 1612–43. Sculptural details from the chapel of the College of St John are incorporated into the building's south elevation. The Principal's House probably dates from the foundation of the college in 1538 and was used as such until 1978. Major remodelling of the library had taken place in 1764–7 under the direction of the local wright James Gardner. It included a heightened upper hall with elegant gallery and large, round-headed windows to the south, and a unifying, neoclassically detailed, polished ashlar façade to the South Street elevation, with a frieze depicting coats of arms of the chancellors of the university.

This plan, signed and dated January 1827, shows the building extended by two bays to the west in an identical style under the direction of the government architect, Robert Reid. A thin red line marks the seamless join. To accommodate the addition it was necessary to demolish an arcaded residence block (erected *c.*1620), and move the entrance porch of St Mary's, which formerly protruded into South Street, to its present position. Reid's work was part of an ambitious scheme for the university's buildings, which included the rebuilding of the United College (with the exception of the college church and the adjoining former residence block), and major remodelling of St Mary's (1828–30), which Reid had originally wanted to demolish, all as recommended in the report of the commissioners for visiting the universities of Scotland, 1826.

Subsequent alterations to the library buildings included the panel bearing the royal arms being extended and moved to its present position on South Street in the 1850s, the removal of the porch from the Principal's House, the creation of ground floor windows in 1891 (although not in accordance with the pencil note made on Reid's drawing) and major internal remodelling of the Senate or Upper West Room in 1899–1901, designed in a 17th-century style by Robert Rowand Anderson. Significant extensions were built to the south in the late 19th and early 20th centuries. The oak panelling, massive stone chimneypiece, and leaded panes in the windows of Parliament Hall were installed in 1930 to the designs of Mills and Shepherd architects, Dundee.

It is a jewel of a building, of much elegance and beauty, which once housed some of the treasured volumes of the nation. It might be regarded as the historic heart of the university and was the public face of its library until the current building in North Street succeeded it in 1976.

Robin D.A. Evetts

8 A Monument Half-finished

Robert Adamson and David Octavius Hill, 'Scott Monument, Edinburgh, during construction', *c.*1844

Salted paper print from calotype negative, 190 × 139mm

Provenance: purchased with generous financial assistance from the National Fund for Acquisitions and the Art Fund, 2005

ALB77–8

David Octavius Hill, artist, joined Robert Adamson, photographer, in 1843 and ignited one of the most creative collaborations in the history of photography. Founded on the production of the calotype, a barely commercial medium, their practice as portrait and topographical photographers nonetheless incubated a powerful public charge. A revolutionary technology became a tool of commemoration: of shattering religious schism in the Great Disruption of 1843; of the 'bourgeois giants' of early Victorian Edinburgh; and of an urban landscape subject to disorientating physical change. In the interpretation of their work, subsequent generations have celebrated the artistry of the calotype, an idea that has too often overshadowed other potential readings. Revisiting our understanding of this material we witness, during the 1840s, the emergence of a technological aesthetic, born from a reproducible medium that struggled for definition as both art and document. For the German critic, Walter Benjamin, writing in the 1930s, Adamson and Hill's photography was characterized by an unprecedented congruence of subject and technique perceived in the technical luminosity of the calotype image. This, described as early photography's 'aura', would soon decay, reduced from the 1860s by the commercialization of an industrialized medium.

The act of photographing monuments, sculpture and public buildings was central to Adamson and Hill's practice, such as in their famous images of tombs from Edinburgh's Greyfriars churchyard. It enabled the key Romantic strategy of mobilizing historic values to critique the present. Their calotype of George Meikle Kemp's half-built Scott Monument, erected between 1841 and 1844, is a strikingly self-referential commentary on the historicity of their present. More so than any other European author, Walter Scott's writing was premised on a concept of epochal historical change. The vast popular identification with his conservative Romanticism lay in its accommodation of past and present, its embracing of capitalist modernity filtered by the values of an earlier age. Edinburgh was now Scott's town, the capital of Romance.

In Adamson and Hill's calotype we get a sense of a city being monumentalized in Scott's image and of the active fabrication of urban space. Kemp's homage to the author not only consolidates myth, but also embodies transcendence and the possibility of imaginative flight. Moreover, a monument half-finished is an historical restitution only partially achieved. A series of photographs of the Scott Monument, including the masons at work, reveals the centrality of this subject to Adamson and Hill's world view. It is the richness of an historicism inspired by Scott that they exploited so subtly in many of their Edinburgh calotypes.

Duncan Forbes

Robert Adamson (R. Adamson & D.O. Hill, 1843–5). ALB21–2 2

9 Pictorial Armchair Exotica

John Thomson, 'A Cyprian Maid', 1878

Woodburytype, 110 × 89mm

Provenance: from *Through Cyprus with a Camera in the Autumn of 1878* (London, 1879); date of acquisition unknown

rf DS54.T5.8

With the global expansion of the British Empire, the Victorian era witnessed a concurrent growth in the market for visual portfolios of distant territories and subjects. The Scottish photographer John Thomson (1837–1921) was at the forefront of this industry in pictorial armchair exotica, producing several deluxe albums of images from foreign countries, most famously *The Antiquities of Cambodia* (1867) and his four-volume masterpiece *Illustrations of China and Its People* (1873–4). 'A Cyprian Maid' is one of 61 photographs reproduced in his two-volume work *Through Cyprus with a Camera in the Autumn of 1878*, published early the following year to considerable critical acclaim. This sumptuous publication exemplifies the topical enterprise of 19th-century commercial photographers and their mediation of Victorian public perceptions of foreign territories and peoples.

After three centuries of Ottoman rule, Cyprus came under British jurisdiction after a treaty signed by the two powers on 4 June 1878. Whether or not Thomson arrived with an official commission to document the newly acquired protectorate is uncertain, but its potential strategic significance for British ambitions in the Middle East underpinned his wider agenda: to produce a visual survey of the island and its inhabitants. In his introduction, Thomson outlined the shift in the island's foreign governance: 'although the island has been woefully wrecked by Turkish maladministration, my readers will perceive that it is neither barren nor "exhausted", and that at no distant day it may regain something at last of its old renown as a centre of commerce in the Levant'. The photographs therefore functioned both as evidence of past neglect and potential future prosperity, marking the pictured sites and subjects as on the verge of renewal under British management.

As an experienced travel photographer, Thomson was well qualified to suggest the notion of a benevolent, albeit unquestioned, imperialist authority in his portfolio. 'A Cyprian Maid' presents a demure, compliant sitter for the viewer's consideration. With her hands carefully arranged in her lap and her eyes averted, Thomson arranged the sitter according to the established conventions of the three-quarter-length portrait. According to the photographer's accompanying text, the anonymous sitter presented 'an ordinary type of the women of Cyprus'. Placed before a monochrome background bereft of social context, she complies with an aesthetic coded for Victorian audiences to denote generic feminine virtue. Given the biblical associations of the island, the sitter assumes a pose reminiscent of Victorian representations of the Madonna. Yet the portrait also draws attention to her ethnographic details and costume, such as the carefully arranged necklaces and embroidered fabrics, in accordance with the contemporary enthusiasm for the social practices and customs of foreign cultures.

Because of its expensive retail price of five guineas, *Through Cyprus with a Camera* found few clients among the prosperous classes of Victorian society. St Andrews is fortunate to possess this important work as part of its significant holdings of John Thomson's work.

Luke Gartlan

Mirifico poteris textos sermone libellos
    Hosce/ operepreciũ perlegere hospes: ades.
Nempe duę currũt vrbes ab origine mũdi:
    Una Cayn: fratris altera structa manu.
Subdolus illã habitat: fraudis reus: ĩprob⁹ oĩs:
    Hanc pius: hanc simplex: pacificusq; pudens.
Illa luto torpet: vitijs corrupta nefandis:
    Hęc delecta manet caraq; sponsa dei.
Sed scelere implicitos manes petit illa ꝓfundos:
    Hęc virtute micans ęthera lęta tenet.
Illa sinistrorsuz vel ad impia tartara tendit:
    Hęc dextro innitens calle: vireta subit.
Hac iter Elysiũ duce puri fronde metalli:
    Illac ditis hiat panda vorago fatim.
Has ter sex libris discreuerat atq; quaternis
    Augustinus: opus forte magister agens.
Falsa etiam excussit cautus figmẽta deoꝝ:
    Confutans verbis dogmata stulta suis.
Quoq; modo primũ regalis machina mundi
    Condita: nil falsis debeat illa deis.
Improbat atq; viros tenuit quos error auit
    Spiritibus partem qui tribuere malis.
Unius impio regitur bene principis orbis.
    Nec fortuna graui nos premit arbitrio.

10 Lost and Found

Augustine of Hippo, *De trinitate* and *De civitate Dei cum commento*, 1489

Basel: Johann Amerbach, 1489

Folio, 321 × 218mm

Provenance: 15th-century inscription of Robert Hindmarsh; probably the copy in St Leonard's College inventory of late 1590s; subsequently lost to the university; reacquired by purchase, 1948

Typ SwB.A89AA

On 7 May 1948 the mediaeval scholar Neil Ker wrote to George Bushnell, university librarian at St Andrews, describing a printed book with early St Andrews inscriptions that he had spotted in a Cambridge bookshop. The asking price was £24, and on 19 May Bushnell wrote to thank Ker for his information and to say that the university had purchased the book. Thus a book that had arrived in St Andrews very soon after its publication returned to its first home.

The year 1489 marked the beginning of a series of editions of the works of St Augustine from the press of Johann Amerbach, which was to culminate in a collected edition of 1505–6. *De trinitate* and *De civitate Dei* were printed as separate works but often bound together, as is the case here. Both titles are inscribed along the volume's fore-edge, indicating that they were together from the 15th century. The books are fine examples of his output; the *De civitate Dei* has a woodcut showing the Cities of God and Satan, in which the angels and demons, one of which is holding an early gun, confront each other.

However, it is the provenance that makes this volume so important for St Andrews. That the book was in Scotland soon after its publication is evident from the signature of its first owner, Robert Hindmarsh, who bequeathed the book to the Augustinian priory in St Andrews. Hindmarsh describes himself as 'professor of sacred theology and canon of the monastery'. He seems to have taught theology to the university students, though whether in the priory itself, St Salvator's College or the Faculty of Theology is uncertain. He died about 1500.

The next owner to sign the book was John Annand. His inscription also describes him as canon of St Andrews, with the right to use the book during his lifetime, by permission of Prior John Hepburn. He must have had the book from Hindmarsh's death onwards and retained it for most of his life. In a 1518 charter Annand was described as 'professor of canon law in the Church of St Andrews', and in 1544 he became principal of St Leonard's College at a time when the Protestant faith was beginning to attract both masters and students. Prior Hepburn had founded St Leonard's College in 1512 to help the Church combat heresy, and the college had a strong connection with the priory until the Reformation. Annand himself remained staunchly Catholic; John Knox called him a 'rottin papist', and indeed in 1547 the two clashed publicly in the parish church. Annand died about 1550.

The library of St Leonard's College was the most comprehensive in the university, thanks largely to the custom whereby masters and canons of the priory presented it with their books. Annand seems to have followed this tradition. That both works were closely read is obvious from the careful and frequent annotations in a number of early hands, including those of both Hindmarsh and Annand.

It is likely that the book was one of those taken from St Andrews to Edinburgh by Dr John Lee when he became principal there in 1840. John Veitch, Professor of Logic, Metaphysics and Rhetoric at St Andrews, bought it at a sale of Lee's books in 1860. Not until Neil Ker discovered it in Pearson's bookshop in Cambridge in 1948, however, did the opportunity again arise to recover it for the University Library.

Christine Gascoigne

11 Six Ages of the World

Werner Rolevinck, *Fasciculus Temporum*, 1478

Cologne: Nicholas Gotz, 1478

Folio, 390 × 280mm

Provenance: ownership inscriptions of William Fowler, Alexander Fraser, 1593, John Leslie and William Guild; from the library of William Guild, bequeathed 1657

World or 'Universal' chronicles were frequently written and copied in the later Middle Ages, but the *Fasciculus Temporum* (Compendium of Times) of Werner Rolevinck was the first to be printed. Rolevinck, from Laer in Westphalia, was a monk at the Carthusian house at Cologne, and it was here that the first edition of his chronicle was printed in 1474. The work proved incredibly popular, and more than 30 further editions were printed before Rolevinck's death in 1502.

Universal histories were compiled to fulfil two principal needs: to provide a 'time-line' of dates, usually beginning with the Creation, and to give an outline of events during the traditional Six Ages of the World. Chronology was of the essence, and it is certainly central to the conception and design of Rolevinck's work. The Creation, he believed, had occurred 5,199 years before the birth of Christ. Following a *tabula brevis* (index), the 'First Age' begins with the six days of Creation and an account of Adam and Eve and their descendants. From this point onwards, in an astonishingly complex and innovative piece of typography, a double line of dates runs through the centre of the entire volume, the upper one counting the years forward from the Creation, the lower one (printed upside down) counting 'backwards' from 5199 BC (*ante Christi nativitatem*) to the birth of Christ in the year AD 1. Rolevinck was the first chronicler extensively to employ a system of BC dating. From the birth of Christ onwards, the two central date-lines record the years since the Creation (*anno mundi*) and the years AD (*anno Christi*). For the content of his history, Rolevinck drew mainly from well-known sources ultimately dependent on the Bible, the imperial history of Martinus Polonus and the *Liber Pontificorum* (Book of Popes). The names of figures such as Old Testament patriarchs, popes and emperors are placed in roundels, and the text is compiled around what was known about them.

How this volume came to Scotland is not clear, but its first owner was evidently William Fouler (or Fowler), whose name appears in blue and red ink in three places and who is probably to be identified as dean of Haddington in the late 15th century. It is likely that he was also the person responsible for adding the feature that makes it unique: the handwritten roundels and notes that run along the lower margin of the folios and relate to early Scottish history. From the 5th century AD onwards, this becomes more detailed and at times strongly partisan. King David I (1124–53) is 'Santus David Rex', the name of William Wallace appears prominently, and a remark by Rolevinck that Scotland was 'a part of England' is struck through with the comment '*falsus est*'. It may also have been Fowler who added the last folio, a brief attempt to continue Rolevinck's chronicle into the 1480s and 1490s.

The text is embellished with red and blue capitals throughout, and there are a number of hand-coloured woodcuts, including illustrations of Noah's Ark and the Tower of Babel, the cities of Rome and Cologne, and the Crucifixion and Resurrection of Christ. According to a series of notes at the front of the *tabula brevis*, the volume was owned successively by Alexander Fraser and John Leslie, bishop of Ross, in the 16th century, and by William Guild, principal of King's College, Aberdeen, in the 17th century. It was Guild who bequeathed it to the Library of St Andrews University in 1657, together with the rest of his books.

Christopher Given-Wilson

Tempus effeminatum incepit circa annos domini mille in quo fides christiana valde cepit deficere et declinare a pristina virilitate vt in prophecia sancte Hildegardis Et in multis regionibus christianitatis nec sacramenta nec ecclesiastici ritus seruabantur auguriis et maleficiis intendentes Et erant sacerdotes sic populus Sed misericors dominus contra hec mala inter plures apostolicos virorum suscitauit qui hanc ariditatem hominis exemplis et predicacionibus irrigaret domino cooperante et sermonem confirmante sequentibus signis Et multi ordines nimio feruore succreuerunt vt periculosum tempus illustraret de quibus consequenter fit mentio. Et quia iam sepe hominum reformaciones facte fuerunt preterea

Imperatores. spe et in sequentibus future sunt ideo fatuum est determinare quando antichristus tunc vel tunc veniet propter maliciam temporis quod plerique attemptarunt: quos omnes fefellit sua opinio et euangelica dei sit sapiencia et ipsa temporis reprobauit experientia Horum errorum immensus est numerus.

Henricus secundus annis 18

Iste Henricus fuit gener Conradi in silua natus cum et hic ad occidendum traditus: sed tamen deo protegente illesus euasit adhuc puer Cum autem imperator esset effectus monasterium edificauit in loco natiuitatis sue Vide pulchram historiam in cronica Martini et Vincencii etc. Hic victoriosus fuit contra ytaliam intrans Pandulphum campanie principem cepit Abbatem Vulderse sedauit qui tunc potestas fuit dyabolo tractante. Hunc dicunt bellicosum fecisse que etiam increpauit.

Gwilhelmus Dimonensis.
Richardus Virdunensis.
Popo Stabulensis.
Helyas Coloniensis
Osbertus Leodicensis
Stephanus Leodicensis
Beruo Augiensis
Omnes isti abbates venerabiles circa hec tempora floruerunt

Fulbertus Carnotensis episcopus in infirmitate visitatur a beata virgine et de eius lacte sanctissimo recreatus est.
Gnotho vir spiritu sapientie et sciencie clarus episcopus Leodicensis.
Heyla auguriatrix in Anglia fuit quam demon de ecclesia extraxit horribiliter
Adelbertus sanctus episcopus Metensis claret
Elbertus abbas Gemelatensis
Bardo vir sanctus episcopus Maguntie claret.

Gwido musicus in ytalia fuit qui inuenit cantum manualem s. per flexuras digitorum notas dinumerando pro pueris informandis.
Egelmotus archiepiscopus Cantuariensis misit brachium sancti Augustini in Angliam eius epistolare habetur

Sanctus Theobaldus vir nobilis de francia inclusus heremita claruit.
Karolphus Merciorum regis filius martirisatus fuit a matertera
Edmundus ex vir sanctus a Danis martirisatus fuit
Corpus gigantis romanorum inuenitur immense magnitudinis incorruptum cum lucerna que non poterat flatu extingui
Statua marmorea erat in apulia cuius caput ostendit thesaurum subaliter
Palumbus presbiter rome fuit nigromanticus contra quem dyabolus orauit et orauit
Monstrum due mulieres in Gallia omnia membra singula vsque ad vmbilicum et diuisim operabantur vna mortua alia supuixit triennio mortuam portans

Anno mundi. 6233. 6283. Almanus. 6243.

Pape

Siluester tercius di. 46	Gregorius 6. an 2. me. 6	Clemens 2us. me. 9 die. 8.	Almanus	Damasus secundus die. 23.	Leo. 9. a. 4. m. 2 die. 6.	Almanus	Victor 2us. an. 2. me. 3.

Anno Christi. 1039. 1048. 1048.

Iste Siluester electus fuit expulso Benedicto sed econtra eiicitur et Benedictus restituitur Quo iterum eiecto Gregorius substituitur qui cum esset rudis litterarum alterum papam ad ecclesiastica officia exequenda secum consecrari fecit Quod cum multis non placeret tercius superinducitur qui solus vices duorum adimpleret Quibus dimicantibus inter se Henricus imperator superueniens omnes deposuit et Clementem secundum substituit a quo statim se coronari fecit promittentibus romanis sine ipsius consensu se nunquam papam electuros Et sic quinque cedentibus sextus institutus est Verum de isto Gregorio Gilbertus dicit quod fuerit vir sanctus et contra Henricum bellum habuit et raptores sancti Petri expulit et cum magno miraculo sit sepultus etc. Vide in cronicis

Iste clemens dictus fuit ante in decretus Bambergensis episcopus qui factus fuit papa per imperatorem propter vnionem reparandam vt iam dictum est.

Iste damasus fuit inuasor ecclesie et subito defunctus est Et statim romani pecierunt sibi dari pontificem sed non teutonicum ad hoc enim non poterant inclinari ex mala consuetudine indurati. Tunc istum Leonem virum sanctum ad hoc inclinauit vt papatum acceptarent: sed postea sibi de hoc fecit conscientiam et resignauit et denuo est electus Hic christum in specie leprosi nocte in lecto suo collocans mane ipsum non inuenit Tandem post laudabilem vitam sancta morte

Iste Victor vir bonus et venerabilis timore imperiali factus est papa sic enim dispositum fuit apostolica sedes hoc tempore quasi viri duplici timore se subtraxerunt s. diuino et humano qui tanto officio se indignos arbitrabantur et tyrannidem romanorum cotidie sustinere timebant.

Quiescens miraculis claret Ipsam multa scripsit et fecit. erat antea episcopus Tulensis et audiuit angelos dicentes Ego cogito cogitaciones pacis dicit dominus.

Sed compellente imperatore quidam nichilominus accesserunt similiter duplici timore Timebant enim deum offendere sic vocati et etiam offensam principis Iste victor multos simoniacos deposuit in consilio Florentino et etiam fornicarios.

De pluralitate beneficiorum que circa hec tempora nimis inualuisse videtur et deinceps continuata multique dolenda ambicione prelatorum et simoniaca labe quod plurima scripta sanctorum patrum habentur detestancia abusiones istas Et nota quod facile inuenti sunt pauperes clerici et doctores qui pluralitatem beneficiorum et pompam ecclesiasticorum reprehenderunt donec offerretur eis occasio participandi Qua accepta conuincitur auaritia excecauit eos Fertur de quodam magistro magne litterature qui valde subtiliter disputauit contra diuitias prelatorum et fastum eorum quasi omnino sic viuere non liceret etc. Hec cum nunciata domino pape fuissent plausibiliter respondit Demus ei bonam preposituram et hec et illa beneficia et bene pacatus erit Factum est ita. Et ecce protinus sententiam mutauit dicens Nunquam intellexi materiam hanc preter modo Quippe qui de inope diues de atepti...

Macabeta Rex

Lulach Rex

Sibilla tiburtina clara habetur que de xp̃o ꝓp

Et augusto respondit ne se deum iuxta stulticiam paganorũ putaret. Et ostendit illi virginem pulcherrim
tenentē puerũ in brachijs et ait. Hic puer maior te est ipsũ adora.

Monarchia romanorum. omniũ maxi

hec tempora incepit. Cũ enim ut testatur iheronim⁹ ꝛ alij sancti doctores per totũ orbem in diuers̃ ꝓuincijs b
lularent subito cunctis mirantibus pacata fuit ꝛ romano pñcipi colla sub miserũt ut aperte domin⁹ deus homi
deret ꝙ illam vniuersalē pacē non bellicus labor sed ipse donasset. Semp vero finito bello aliud successit aut p
orꝗ scissura sequebatur sed xp̃i natiuitate ꝓpinquante vrbs quieuit et orbis.

Reges iudee

herodes ascalonita ã. 3A.

Iste herodes ydumeus primus rex aligenigena apud iudeos fuit. Eius hys
magister diligēter ꝓsequit̃. Et refert eũ fuisse virũ strennuũ ꝛ fide dignũ ꝛ in
notabiliter se habuit. Gratus valde romanis ꝛ popul' qui pacē amabãt. Multa
opa memorabilia fecit Vez i senectute sua cum nimis vellet placere romanis ꝛ audiss̃ de ortu xp̃i timēs belli c
tanꝗ alienigena mirabilit' defecit sensu ꝛ antiqua ꝓbitate amissa innocētes occidit ꝛ plures de filijs suis. Ta
nibus odiosus morbo inualescente flebili morte destituitur ꝛc

Maria nascit̃ anno añ xp̃i natiuitatē. 16. vel circa.

Hystoria euãgelica oĩm scriptu rarũ sanctissima hic texit̃.

Anno mũdi. 4149. — 4199.

Linea xp̃i

Anteꝗ̃ conuenirēt inuē ta est in vtero hñs de spiritusancto hanc pre dixit ysaias ꝓpheta.

Joseph sponsus

Maria mr̃ xp̃i

Zacharias ꝛ elizabeth fuerũt ãbo sc̃e vite qui fuerũt pn̄tes sancti iohis baptiste.

Ioachi ꝛ ãna clarēt sãctitate vite ꝙ post singl'ari grã meruerũt ꝓcreare florē toci⁹ felicitatis mariã oĩm creaturaꝝ excellētissimam que deũ nobis genuit.

Burgũdiones orti sũt gens semp val'da sic dcã qz sup renũ fluuiũ burgos plures habent.

Marc⁹ agrippa gener octauiani sup rēnũ ciuitatē agrippinã cõdidit ꝙ post dcã ē colonia.

Anno mũdi. 4159. ipse ē p̃m⁹ añ xp̃i natiuitatē cũ iã eēt desposat
tia ioseph missus ē angel⁹ gabriel a p̃re lũinũ deo toci⁹ cõsolac
ad ipaz ut ãnũtiaret ei ꝙ veniret pleitudo tp̃is ꝓ reconciliacõe hũa
neris ꝛ ꝙ p ipaz dei fili⁹ hũc mũdũ intrare vellet. Hec igitur om
secreto ꝝ secretissimũ. mirabiliũ mirabilissimũ. salubriũ saluber
desiderabiliũ desiderabilissimũ misterio ꝝ ꝓfundissimũ circa hec
diu expectata adĩpletũ ē ut de⁹ hõ fieret. Quis audiuit vnꝗ̃ si
O si sapiat istud in palato mentis nostre. Vide deuotissimam h
storiam luce p̃mo.

Iohes baptista nascit̃ ꝙ nemo maior int' natos mulierũ surrexit.

TTm̄

in flore Et numerati sunt ciues eius et descripti nonagesies trecentamilia ⁊ ·80· milia· ¶ Mūd⁹ describiť vni
e mādato augusti qđ misterio ñ caruit qꝛ ille nasciť ī mūdo q̄ electos suos ascribē venit ī eťnitate :vt dic̄ Greg⁹·
¶ Valerius maximus fuit hoc tp̄e vir magne fame.

ores romani p hāc lineā ↄtinuāť q̄ oēs augusti dicāť xp̄ē singularē hui⁹ augusti excellēciā Justū eq̄dez ē vt ille
one tbuat q̄ cūctis viuēdi formā ⁊ ēgēdi normā ↄstituit Tāta siq̄dez ī eo ꝓbitas ac strēnuitas emicuit vt vix
ile sit ꝙ vnq̄ destituta natuā hūana discurs⁹ talē edē potuerit Quid vltē xp̄m cū bñdcā mrē sua vidē meruit q̄si
nceri⁹ extiterit vocacōis gēciū ⁊c̄· nec vnq̄ p⁹ hec dñs vōri voluit Araz ei p̄m⁹ extruxit· humilitatꝭ· clemēte· cui
vacāe· discipline ⁊c̄· q̄ ratissime ī tāta sblimitate ↄueniūt exēplar ipē fuit· Bellū ñ ñ coactus accepit Ait ei· Mag
spēdiū aureo hamo pisces cape· qꝛ hami pditi dānū nulla pōt captura pisciū ↄpari Detrahētibꝫ sibi ait ·Jn libera
e liberas eē decz liguas Milites ociari neq̄q̄ ā deliciari pmittebat q̄re ꝓfessio īstitūta ē ad laborē Filias suas ī la
fecit istrui xp̄ē mutabilitatē tpaliū Medi te xēdiq; ñ solū artē ꝫ vsū hēbat Nec ad se ñ vultu maturo si oī vestitu
itate accedē pmittebat Regna q̄ iure belli q̄sierat ꝑter pauca reddidit ā alienis benigne tribuit Testē se ī iudicijs
gari ⁊ repelli cq̄missimo āno patiebať ·Plures hūit sibi marie familiares q̄ cū meli⁹ poterāt eū extiguere etiam
cis bellis necebanť Alij tee q̄terq; piuri cū grāz poscerēt vitā et bō ab ipō ipetraꝛt O q̄ multi fuerūt q̄ se de sā no
nguine ꝓgenitos gloriabanť ꝫ mores nō imitabanť·

uratores iudee	Archela us ānis ·9·	Compo nius·	Marcus
¶ Fili⁹ herodis Sub eo dñs redijt ex egipto		Hic loco archelai substitutus est	Sub isto moritur salome soror he rodis

Hic icipit sexta etas

Xp̄s dñs ex maria vgine nasciť anno mūdi ·4199· completo·

Mundi hūana vsq3 ad finale iudiciū hūs an nos quot nouit de⁹

s nasciť·	4200
ra xp̄i	
o dñi·	·1·

tus est circa hec tpa dominus noster de virgine pura nouo
ne fm ꝓphetica ꝓmissa Et hec ē pleitudo temporis de quo
olus dicit quādo misit deus filiū suū in mundū Ob hoc in
hic sexta etas mundi cuius finē solus deus nouit Et dicit
ustinus ꝙ hec etas dicāť senectus que sexe extenditur vltra
es precedentes etatesꝭ qꝛ pleriq; hominū viuunt etiā vsq3
entum viginti ānos aut vltra et notū ē ꝙ sexagenarios se
vocamus Vnde fatuū ē velle determinare quātitatē eius·
res ei hoc attēptarūt q̄ oēs fuere decepti sicut ꝓbat doctor
tus ⁊c̄

xp̄ianoꝝ p̄ncipalissima oīm etatū notissima cēleberrimaq3
ē ān⁹ octauiani ⁊c̄·Olimpiadis cētesimenonagesime ter
Et fm bedā ānus mūdi·4199·ↄpletus· vniuersꝭ Vnū tolle
ad milia q̄nq; ducētis Nascēti dño beda dat a prothopla
Jēe ān xp̄m duo·ce·min⁹ vno milia q̄nq3 Et h tāq̄ ꝓbabi
mod⁹ ab ecc̄ia seruaťt et ē magisꝭ vulgatusꝭ Sūt ⁊ alij diu
odi supputacōnū q̄dā breuioresꝭ vt hebreoꝝ q̄dā lōgioresꝭ
methodij ⁊ aliorū de q̄bꝫ imēsus ē labor tractare vtilitas m
modica Vide singula locis suis ⁊c̄·

¶ De principatu romano sic dicit cicero in libro de offi
cijs· Certum est fuisse aliquod tempus quo sine regi
bus viuebaťt ·At postq̄ iure gentiū possessiones ce ꝑ
runt diuidi: non alia de causa rēges instituti sunt nisi
iusticie fruende Nam cum in inicio premeretur mul
titudo ab hijs qui majores opes habebant ad vnum
aliquē virū confugiebant virtute prestantem qui ꝓ
hiberet iniuriari tenuiores equitatem cōstituendo su
mos cum infimisꝭ pari iure pertingeret Cunq; adhuc
regnantibꝫ regibusꝭ debiliores nonnūq̄ opprimeren
tur: leges constitui placuit que ad iudicandū nō odio
aut gratia ducerentur· sed tales inopi qualesꝭ potenti
prestarent aures ·Quo fit vt leges non solum popu
lum· sed regem quoq3 obligare sciamus· At si regē
contemnere legesꝭ· rapere bona subditorū· violaťe vir
ginesꝭ stupraťe matronas ⁊ cetēra illicita facere videa
mus · Nūquid illo submisso alius sublimabiť qui et
bene gubernare ⁊ legibꝫ nouit obtemperare· .

12 A Pictorial Chronicle of a Remarkable Life

Hamish M. Brown, 'The Quirang Needle', 1996

Transparency, 35mm
Provenance: from the H.M. Brown Collection, gift of the photographer, 2005–9
Uncatalogued

A lone, bowed figure unconcernedly steps down across the scree in the shadow of the crumbling cliffs that delineate the Trotternish Ridge on the Isle of Skye. This is a contorted land where it is possible to imagine that 'here be monsters' dwelling in deep crevices within the grasp of the crags. Close by, a huge profiled face has been sculpted from solidified molten rock, creating its own brooding presence. This is an image captured by someone who appreciates where he is.

Known as the Quirang, this bizarre landscape is the most prominent feature on the northern end of a 20-mile-long lava sheet escarpment that undulates towards the tilted springboard of The Storr, invitingly framed in the centre of the picture. This is not a gentle landscape of slow weathering; it is, instead, the site of a catastrophic slumping collapse where massive sections of the cliff edge have freed themselves to slide across the underlying sedimentary strata. These curious rock features, still steadily shedding tiny stones that pepper the slopes beneath, remain as a relic of an ancient landslip and stand in ranks below the main escarpment edge. The leaning pinnacle of the Quirang Needle, with its twisted cap, guards an entrance that breaches the castellated walls into a forbidding fortress. Within lurks a high hidden green sward known as 'The Table', while on one flank sits 'The Prison', a dark hulk of rock. It is a strange and mysterious place to wander at will.

It would not be inappropriate if the picture's solitary figure was the photographer himself, whose stravaiging life has taken him intimately through the endless variety of the Scottish landscape. Hamish Brown (the recipient both of an MBE and of a St Andrews DLitt degree) has spent a lifetime tramping wild and mountainous places and has rewarded those who read his books and poems with unique insights into his homeland. For example, his succinct account in *Hamish's Mountain Walk* of a solo continuous journey on foot, by canoe and by bicycle in 1974, traversing all of the Scottish Munros, bewitches the reader into absorbing the writer's relish in wandering his highland hills. This pioneering epic journey was his seventh round of the Munros, a feat that only the dedicated achieve even once. He has not, however, restricted himself to his native landscape. He has climbed, explored and photographed in the Alps, Corsica and other more well-trodden uplands, but his greatest attachment for almost half a century has been to the dry, bare, high hills and the indigenous residents of the Atlas Mountains in Morocco. In 1995 he fulfilled a longstanding ambition to trek their ancient paths for over 900 miles, from close to the Atlantic Ocean to where the mountain chain delves into the depths of the eastern desert.

Although often he travelled alone, he has nonetheless played a key role in inspiring others with a love for their natural environment, most significantly when in his early days as a pioneer of outdoor education he enabled the underprivileged children of the innovative Braehead School at Leven, in fading industrial Fife, to discover for themselves what the great expanse of the natural world had to offer.

The photography of Hamish Brown, so generously donated by him to the library, is an addition to the collections that not only impresses through its visual virtuosity but is also a pictorial chronicle of a remarkable life steeped in many landscapes and cultures.

Philip Gribbon

13 For the Admiration of After Ages

John Duns Scotus, *Quaestiones in quatuor libros Sententiarum* and *Quodlibeta*, 1481

Nuremberg: Anton Koberger, 1481
Folio, 398 × 279mm
Provenance: gift of Patrick Young, 1614
Typ GN.A81KD

In the Conventual Church of the Franciscan Friars in Cologne stands a white stone sarcophagus containing the remains of Blessed John Duns Scotus. On one side is inscribed a Latin epitaph, which translates as 'Scotland begot me, England received me, France taught me, Cologne holds me'.

There are few early documents testifying to dates and places in Scotus's life, but in 1521 the Scottish philosopher John Mair (provost of St Salvator's College, 1534–50) wrote in his *History of Greater Britain*: 'John Duns, that subtle doctor, was a Scottish Briton, for he was born at Duns, a village eight miles distant from England, and separated from my own home [Haddington] by seven or eight leagues only.' We know that Duns Scotus was ordained (very aptly) at St Andrew's Priory in Northampton in 1291. This puts his birth sometime around 1265. Mair reports that Scotus studied and debated in Oxford, where he became a Franciscan, then in Paris, and that he later went to Cologne where he died, 'while still a young man'. The last mention of him is his signature on a document dated February 1308, and it is supposed that he died later that year, aged 43.

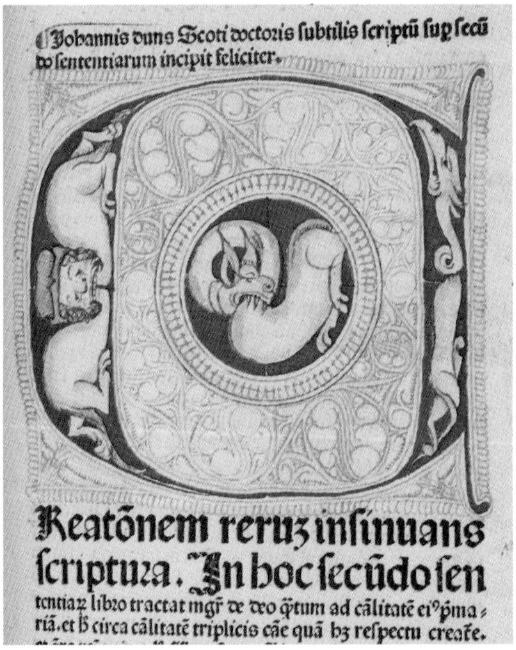

Mair also writes that Duns 'left behind him [in Oxford] for the admiration of after ages … four books on the *Sentences* … and produced [in Paris] another set of lectures on the *Sentences*, more compendious and more useful [which] we have but lately caused to be printed with metal types [Paris, 1518]'.

The Four Books of Sentences is the most famous textbook of the Middle Ages, a 'reader' compiled by Peter Lombard (1100–60) of selected passages from the Bible, early church fathers and mediaeval theologians. It was used as the basis for studying and lecturing throughout the mediaeval colleges and universities, and many leading scholars wrote commentaries on it. The present text is mostly based on Scotus's Oxford commentary, edited in 1477 by the English scholar Thomas Penketh and published in this edition in 1481. It is a large folio, printed in 'black letter' type in double columns, with beautifully illuminated and decorated capitals at the beginning of each part. The dragon-like creature biting itself (an *ouroboros*) is a common motif in earlier illustrated manuscripts.

The book was printed in Nuremberg and bound in calf over oak boards in the workshop of the publisher, Anton Koberger. It is heavily annotated in a variety of early hands, and this edition, if not this copy, was well known to John Mair, who consulted it in the preparation of his own *Sentences* commentary of 1519. Thus are linked two of the great Scottish philosophers of the pre-modern period, and more than five centuries later this edition of Scotus remains available to be studied by contemporary scholars.

John Haldane

¶ Johannis duns Scoti ordinis minorum doctoris precellentissimi scriptum super primo Sententiarum incipit feliciter.

Cupiētes aliquid de penuria et cetera.

Circa prologum hui9 primi libri sententiarū querunt̄ quinq̃. Primum de necessitate hui9 doctrine. 7 spectat ad gen9 cause efficiētis. 7 est questio. Utrū necessariū sit homini ꝓ statu isto aliquā doctrinā specialē supnaturalit̄ īspirari. Scd̄m spectat ad gen9 cause formalis. 7 est questio Utrū cognitō supnaturalis necessaria viatori. tradita sit sufficiēter in sacra scriptura. Terciū spectat ad genus cause materialis. 7 ē questio. Utrū theologia sit d̄ deo tanq̃ de subiecto pmo. Quartum 7 quintū ptinēt ad gen9 cause finalis. 7 ē quarta q̄stio. Utrū theologia sit practica. quinta vō questio. Utrū ex ordine ad praxim vt ad finem dicatur p se scientia practica.

Primo queritur vtrū homini

ꝓ statu isto sit necessariū aliquā doctrinā specialem supnaturaliter inspirari ad quā videlicz nō possit attingere lumine naturali intellect9. Et videt̄ q̄ nō. sic. Omnis potētia habēs aliqd̄ ꝯmūe ꝓ pmo obiecto naturali pōt in qd̄libet ꝯtentū sub illo sicut in p se obiectum naturale. Hoc ptz p exemplū de pmo obiecto visus 7 alijs ꝯtentis sub illo. 7 ita inductiue in alijs obiectis primis 7 potētijs. Patet etiā p ratōez. q2 primuz obiectū dicit̄ qd̄ est adequatū potētie: ꝫ si in aliq̃ esset ratō ei9 circa qd̄ nō posset potētia habē actū naturaliter. nō esset potētie adequatū ꝫ excederet potētiā. patz ergo maior. Sed primū obiectū intellect9 nr̄i naturale est ens inq̄ntū ens. ergo intellect9 nr̄ pōt naturalit̄ habere actū circa qd̄cūq̃ ens 7 sic circa qd̄cūq̃ intelligibile. etiā circa nō ens. q2 negatō cognoscit̄ p affirmationem. ḡ 7c̄. ꝓbatio minoris. Auic. pmo metaph. c. v. Ens 7 res pma impssione impmunt̄ in aīam. nec possunt manifestari ex alijs. Si autē esset aliqd aliud ab istis pmū obiectū. ista possent manifestari p ratōem illius. ꝫ hoc ē impossibile. ḡ. ¶ Preterea. sensus nō indiget aliqua cognitōne supnaturali ꝓ isto statu. ḡ nec intellect9. aīs ptz. ꝓbatio ꝯñe. Natura nō deficit in necessarijs. iij. de aīa. 7 si in impfectis nō deficit. mlto magis nec in pfectis. ḡ si nō deficit in potētijs inferioribꝫ q̄ntum ad necessaria eis ꝓpter act9 suos habendos 7 finē eaꝝ ꝯsequēdū. multomagis nō deficit in necessarijs potētie supiori ad actū suū 7 finē ꝯsequēdū. ḡ 7c̄. ¶ Preterea si aliqua talis doctrina sit necessaria. ꝫ ē q2 potētia in puris naturalibꝫ ē iproportionata obiecto vt sic cognoscibili. ḡ optet q̄ p aliqd aliud a se fiat ei ꝓportionata. illud aliud aut ē naturale aut supnaturale. si ē naturale. ḡ totū est īproportionatū obiecto primo. si supnaturale. ḡ potētia est īproportionata illi. et ita sequit̄ q̄ p aliud optet ei ꝓportionari. 7 sic ī infinitum. cū ergo nō sit ꝓcedere ī infinitū. ij. metaph. optet stare in pmo. dicēdo q̄ potētia intellectiua sit ex se ꝓportionata omni cognoscibili. et ꝫm omnem modum cognoscibilis. quare 7c̄.

Ad oppositū. ij. thimo. iij.

Omnis scriptura diuinit9 inspirata vtilis ē ad docendum. ad arguendū 7c̄. ¶ Preterea Baruch. iij. de sapientia dicit̄. Nō est q possit scire vias ei9. ꝫ q scit vniuersa nouit eā. ḡ nullus ali9 pōt habere eā nisi a sciēte vniuersa ꝫ q̄tum ad necessitatē de facto. subdit. Tradidit eā Jacob puero suo 7 isrl̄ dilecto suo. ꝫ q̄tuz ad vet9 testamentū. 7 sequit̄. Post ꝫ in terris visus ē 7 cū hoībꝫ ꝯuersat9 ē. s. qn̄ tradidit eā q̄ ad nouū testāmtū.

In ista questione videtur

esse ꝯtrouersia inter phos 7 theologos. tenent eīn phi pfectionē nature 7 negāt pfectionē supnaturalē. Theologi vō cognoscūt defectū nature 7 necessitatē gratie 7 pfectionū supnaturaliū. Diceret ḡ phus q̄ nulla est cognitō supnaturalis homi necessaria ꝓ isto statu. sed q̄ oēm noticiā sibi necessariā posset acqrere ex actōne causaꝝ naturaliuz. ¶ Ad ꝫ adducit̄ sil' auctoritas 7 ratio phi ex diuersis locis. pmo p illud. iij. de aīa. vbi dicit q̄ intellect9 agens est q̄ est oīa facere. 7 intellect9 possibilis est q̄ est oīa fieri. Ex ꝫ arguit̄ sic. actiuo naturali 7 passiuo debite approximatis 7 non impeditis necessario sequit̄ actio. q2 nō dependet essentialit̄ nisi ab eis tāq̃ a causis prioribꝫ. Actiuū aūt respectu omniū intelligibiliū est intellect9 agens. 7 passiuū est ītellect9 possibilis. 7 hec sunt naturalit̄ in aīa. nec sūt impedita. ptz ergo v̄tute naturali istoꝝ pōt seq act9 intelligendi respectu cuiuscūq̃ intelligibilis. ¶ Cōfirmat̄ ratō. omī potētie passiue naturali correspondet aliqd̄ actiuū naturale. aliogn videret̄ potētia passiua eē frustra ī natura si p nihil ī natura posset reduci ad actū. sed intellect9 possibilis ē potentia passiua 7 naturalis respectu quoꝝcūq̃ intelligibilium ḡ correspōdet sibi aliqua potentia actiua naturalis. sequit̄ ḡ ꝓpositū. minor ptz. q2 intellect9 possibilis naturalit̄ appetit cognitionē cuiuscūq̃ cognoscibilis. naturaliter etiā pficit̄ p quācūq̃ cognitōez. ergo ē naturalit̄ receptiu9 cuiuscūq̃ intellectōis. ¶ Preterea. vj. metaph. diuidit̄ scientia speculatiua ī metaphisicā 7 phisicā siue naturalez 7 mathematicā. Et ex ꝓbatōe hui9 ibidē nō videt̄ possibile plures eē habit9 speculatiuos. q2 in istis ꝯsideratur de toto ente 7 in se 7 q̄ ad oēs ptes ei9. sicut aūt nō posset eē aliqua alia sciētia speculatiua ab istis. sic nec practica aliq̃ alia a practicis acq̄sitis actiuis 7 factiuis. ergo scie practice acq̄site sufficiūt ad pficiendū intellectū practicū. 7 speculatiue acq̄site sufficiūt ad pficiendū intellectū speculatiuū. ¶ Preterea potens naturalit̄ intelligē principiū. pōt naturalit̄ cognoscere 7 intelligē ꝯclusiones inclusas ī principio. Hanc ꝓbo. q2 sciētia ꝯclusionū nō depēdet nisi ex intellectu principij 7 ex deductōe ꝯclusionū ex pricipio. sicut ptz ex diffinitōe scire pmo posterioꝝ. ꝫ deductō ē ex se manifesta. sicut ptz ex diffinitōe sillogismi pfecti pmo prioꝝ q2 nulli9 est indigēs vt appareat euidēter necessari9. ergo si pricipia intelligūt̄ 7 deductō manifesta ē ex se habent̄ oīa que sūt necessaria ad sciam ꝯclusionis. ptz ergo maior. Sed naturalit̄ intelligim9 pricipia pma in quibꝫ v̄tualiter includūtur oēs ꝯclusiones scibiles. ergo naturalit̄ possum9 scire oēs ꝯclusiones istas scibiles. ꝓbatō prime ptis minoris. q2 termini primoꝝ pricipioꝝ sūt coīssimi. ergo istos possum9 naturalit̄ intelligere. q2 ex pmo phisicoꝝ coīssima a nobis pmo intel-

14 Corporate Identity

Matrix of university seal, 1414–18

Brass, 80mm diameter, single-sided with central spine on reverse
Provenance: commissioned by the university
UYUY103

The possession of a seal is integral to the corporate identity of any institution. It is used to authenticate documents recording the acts and decisions of that body and is a visible guarantee of veracity. So the decision of the University of St Andrews on 8 December 1414 to commission a seal marks a significant point in its early history.

An engraved matrix or die would usually include an image and suitable inscription of ownership. The legend reads: *sigillum universitatis doctorum magistrorum et scolarium sancti andree* (the seal of the doctors, masters and scholars of the university of Saint Andrew – or 'St Andrew's University'). It is not possible to date the matrix precisely, but it is accepted that its heraldic references predate the change of allegiance of the university from the schismatic Pope Benedict XIII; thus it was made some time between 1414 and 1418.

A matrix was incised or hollowed out, and the lettering was engraved in reverse so that the wax impression – or seal – created using it would bear a legible inscription and image. Relatively few mediaeval wax seals survive entirely intact since they are inherently vulnerable: damage occurs to the wax through friction and temperature, and the heavy seal has often been torn away from the tag that attached it to the document.

Central to this seal is the figure of St Andrew on his cross. Below the saint is a rare visual representation of academic life in the mediaeval institution: a class of seven scholars along with a regent at his desk accompanied by the 'luminator' sitting with a lantern. Alternatively, this has been said to portray a rectorial court, with the seated official attended by the bedellus carrying the mace that habitually accompanied the rector on his official duties. Above is a triple canopy bearing three coats of arms, describing in heraldic form the founders of the university. These are Pope Benedict XIII, King James I and Bishop Henry Wardlaw. Elements from the shields of all three founders – the crescent moon, the lion rampant and the diamonds (mascles) – were incorporated within the first official matriculation of arms of the University of St Andrews in 1905. This was extended and matriculated afresh in 2006 so as to include the motto *aien aristeuein* (ever to excel) with St Andrew and a lion as supporters.

Impressions were made with this seal matrix for many years, being affixed to documents issued by the university, including degree parchments such as that awarded to Thomas James who graduated Master of Arts in 1626. The matrix's engraving has also been adapted for many uses by the university since its commissioning, and versions are to be found embossed in gold on bookbindings and printed on bookplates, on letterheads and even as a logo. There are two other seal matrices in the muniment collection: the second seal of St Salvator's College (silver, *c.*1560) and St Mary's College (brass, *c.*1580). This seal, however, the earliest symbol of the university's corporate identity, is an item of immense significance.

Rachel Hart

15 A Careful Process of Trial and Error

Notebook by Douglas Dunn, 1979–83

Paper, 300 × 208mm

Provenance: from the papers of Douglas Dunn, purchased with generous financial support from the Friends of the National Libraries and Professor Kay Redfield Jamison, 2007

ms38640/50/1

In 2007 the library secured the purchase of the private papers of the poet Douglas Dunn, who was Professor of English at St Andrews from 1991 until his retirement in 2008. Born in Clydeside in 1942, Dunn has published 11 volumes of his own poetry, in addition to collections of short stories, essays and anthologies. He has been awarded several prestigious literary prizes, including the Whitbread Book of the Year prize in 1985 for *Elegies*, an intensely moving collection of poems written after the death of his first wife, Lesley. Dunn was made Fellow of the Royal Society of Literature in 1981 and was awarded an OBE in 2003.

Dunn's eminence as a poet made this an extremely fortunate acquisition. The sheer scale of the archive is staggering: more than 170 box files contain a wealth of material, including correspondence, unpublished poems, stories and essays, working notes, juvenilia, play scripts, and drafts and revisions of many of Dunn's published poems, from all stages of his long career, and there is more to come. In an age of digital media, this collection is all the more remarkable, and it may turn out to be one of the last paper literary archives of size and significance to be acquired by a British university. Indeed, it is so large that its contents are not yet fully known, although it is clear that the archive provides a uniquely detailed insight into the working life, practices and network of collaboration of a major British contemporary writer.

Already identified as one of the collection's great jewels is the garnet-coloured, unlined A4 notebook featured here, in which Dunn composed and redrafted poetry from late 1979 until 1983. In this notebook one can observe in great intimacy the careful process of trial and error, false start and revision, by which a number of poems from *St Kilda's Parliament* and *Elegies*, two of Dunn's most lauded volumes, gestated and gradually evolved towards publication. The picture shows part of the second stage of composition (over six leaves in the notebook) of what later becomes the *St Kilda*'s poem 'War Blinded'. Here titled 'Men Going Home', the poem is already in the a-b-a-b rhyming quatrains of its final form, although many of the stanzas were later discarded or substantially altered. On the previous leaf the earliest version of the poem was untitled, in blank verse, and recognizable only from its subject material (the return of World War I veterans from the trenches) and by the wording of the final line, part of which is retained in the published version: 'Remembering that day when his right hand | Gripped the shoulder of the man in front.' It is noticeable that while in draft the poem's speaker claims to have felt 'as if I'd known that worst of hells', the final version sees him admit, 'That war's too old for me to understand | How he might think', and shifts emphasis from images of the horror of the trenches to images of the nursing home in which a single veteran spends his final days. That Dunn surrenders in this way the author's privilege of appropriating others' experience is typical of his tact as a poet, and it reminds us, as does the ruthlessness of his cancellation marks, that writing is as much about giving up as it is about possession. Given up into the possession of the University Library, this matchless treasure will have much more to teach us yet about the production and processes of poetry.

Chris Jones

~~Pity the poor surveyors, rushed motorists,~~
~~Who know too clearly what they do~~

~~Late for my train, half drunk and weighted down~~
~~With a briefcase and an armful of parcels,~~

MEN GOING HOME

As the train raced, it gradually ~~was~~ grew clearer
That on the lit edge of ~~the~~ they blurred passing lines,
A long thin multitude was strung out there
~~Through tunnels, on embankments, by birches and pines~~
By towns and tunnels and by gaunt plantations.

It was not hard to fall into their lives
In one sore summary ~~from carriage doors~~ of pain and grief,

As if in me a residue survives
Which cures my cynicism ~~with belief~~ of disbelief.

The more I looked, the clearer they became,
These men strung out in wounded uniforms,
Whose winked insignia were as sly as shame
~~That queue of bodies, faces, legs and arms.~~

Along that queue of bodies, legs and arms

16 'A Very Nice Class of Girls'

Presentation album for Louisa Lumsden, 1900

Art board, 255 × 380mm, in binding embossed with university seal
Provenance: gift of Miss W. Lumsden, 1993
ms38672

The charming testimonial album presented to Louisa Lumsden in 1900 to commemorate her period of office as the first warden of University Hall marks a significant stage in the acceptance of women as full members of the university. Although Elizabeth Garrett (later to become the first British woman to qualify as a doctor) attempted to join the university in 1862, her matriculation was ruled illegal by the University Senatus, and it was to be a further three decades before women were admitted as full-time students. From 1877 the Lady Literate in Arts (LLA) scheme had allowed women to take university examinations at many centres throughout the UK and abroad, and, in anticipation of the admission of women as matriculated students from 1892, an LLA fund was set up to build a hall of residence. University Hall was opened in 1896. This album, prepared by Maclure, Macdonald & Co. of Glasgow, contains photographs of the hall and its public rooms as well as of the residents between 1896 and 1900, set among beautiful watercolour borders. The centrepiece of the album, however, is a lavish address to the first warden signed by 47 of those residents, including 14 of the first female graduates.

In the address, her students noted how well Louisa Lumsden's character and experience, as well as her 'wide, though unobtrusive, learning', had equipped her for the post that she was now relinquishing. Louisa Lumsden was, indeed, a pioneer of women's education. One of the first students, and later the classical tutor, of Girton College, Cambridge, she became, between 1879 and 1882, the founding headmistress of St Leonards School in St Andrews. She saw the invitation to establish a hall of residence within the university as an opportunity to bring to Scotland some of the advantages of the English system of higher education for women. The difficulties that faced her are revealed by Principal James Donaldson's scornful opinion that 'those students who had the old independent Scottish spirit would, of course, go into lodgings, while those students who liked would prefer conventual rule under Miss Lumsden'. The effort of fitting out University Hall almost single-handed, attempts to placate resentful town students and constant disputes with the governing committee of the hall affected her health and led to her resignation.

The presentation of the album at a tea party in June 1900 was described in *College Echoes* as 'the event of the summer session'. In her response Louisa Lumsden thanked her students for the loyalty and sympathy expressed in the address, which revealed that they had entered into 'the very spirit and essence' of her work at University Hall. She had expected a tribute from hall residents, but a letter signed by 70 non-resident women students expressing their appreciation of what she had done for the whole body of students was an agreeable surprise.

Although it did not become a 'Scottish Girton', University Hall, the first purpose-built hall of residence for women in Scotland, was an undoubted success. Even Principal Donaldson had to admit in 1909 that it attracted 'a very nice class of girls ... with great benefit to the whole university'. At the celebrations of the 500th anniversary of the foundation of the university in 1911 Louisa Lumsden finally received the recognition she deserved in the form of an honorary degree. In 1925 she was appointed DBE for her services to education. She died, aged 94, in 1935.

Ann J. Kettle

Address

from the Students of University Hall
St. Andrews,

To

Louisa Innes Lumsden,

Warden of University Hall.

We, who have been Students of University Hall desire, on the occasion of your retirement from the post of Warden, to testify in emphatic terms our gratitude for all that you have done on our behalf, and to express our deep sense of the direct influence which your life and character and your wide, though unobtrusive, learning have made you strong to exercise upon the culture and development of all who came in contact with you. That onerous office whose duties you are now, to our deep regret, relinquishing could have been filled by few women so well endowed by nature, by yet fewer equally equipped by previous experience.

MACLURE MACDONALD & Co GLASGOW.

Senior Students
and
Hall Tutor.

17 An Evocative Blur of Activity

Three photographs by John Edward Aloysius Steggall: 'Clova – Ruined Houses', 1895; 'Horning Sheep in Glen Prosen', 1897; 'Burano – Lace Workers', 1906

Prints, each 93 × 119mm
Provenance: from the J.E.A. Steggall Collection, bequeathed 1935
JEAS-12-7; JEAS-13-37; JEAS-31-42

A man dressed for trekking stands, with almost aggressive directness, on a desolate road, trees hovering over his right shoulder, with mountains looming in the background. Through the foliage a jumble of rough-hewn stones tells us that people used to live here; but the land is quiet now, save for the inquiring visitor. This photograph was taken in 1895 by John Steggall. By this time the camera was a commercial success, portrait studios were dominating the high streets, and the globe was being plundered for images of far-flung exoticism. This image is from Glen Clova in Angus, known for its picturesque beauty and alpine flora. Steggall was an amateur photographer rather than a professional, just one of many who visited the 'five glens' on a tour popularized by the romance of Walter Scott's work and Queen Victoria's passion for highland Scotland. Accordingly, in this image the harsh qualities of rural life are erased by the soft focus of the lens. The brutality

of the enforced clearance of entire communities from these lands only a few generations earlier, to make way for more profitable sheep-farming, are bleached out by this record of sun-streaked solitude. This can also be seen illustrated in 'Horning Sheep in Glen Prosen', where an evocative blur of activity in the sheep pen, with the shaggy-bearded keepers squinting through the glare of midday, is contrasted with the tranquillity of wide open spaces behind. Once more Steggall's photographs illustrate the imposed shift away from the traditional practice of crofting and the resulting local cultural transformation.

While Steggall's photographs were for private albums, they do reflect an attitude to the land that is part of the ethic of empire: the camera as the dominating eye claiming ownership over people and places. In another photograph taken while he was travelling in Italy, Steggall has posed a group of lace-workers, mostly children, who stare into the camera wide-eyed and bemused. The lengthy exposure has blurred anything that moves, but the image clearly captures the lives of the 'other', constructing something that anthropologist Elizabeth Edwards has called a 'cultural theatre'. According to Edwards, this is 'a presentation which constitutes a performative or persuasive act directed towards a conscious beholder'. A staged anecdote of Italian working life is being played out for the viewer, reinforcing a curiosity about how 'others' lead their lives. This is a narrative that Steggall himself would have learned from the contemporary guidebooks and published views of foreign places that reinforced the climate of colonialism.

Born in London, Steggall became Professor of Mathematics and Natural Philosophy at University College, Dundee, in 1883. He was at the pinnacle of his career while taking these photographs. According to his obituary in the *Proceedings of the Edinburgh Mathematical Society*, it was his aim to use 'a few master strokes' to put 'the whole essence of each question into a nutshell'. It was said that he gave the same 'devastating treatment to questions outside mathematics; simplicity and frankness dictating a clear answer which would be given fearlessly'. It is this propensity for succinct detail that must have attracted Steggall to photography, for it was seen as a rational and scientific art.

A vast array of buildings, mountains, valleys and rivers are featured among Steggall's 46 family albums held by the library, and the photographs typify the increasingly mobile middle-class citizen at the turn of the 20th century. While private albums reflect personal relationships and link moments of travel to create a lifetime of nostalgia for their creators, the individual photographs reveal wider cultural attitudes. As viewers we look through the lens with Steggall and can see how men of his stature saw the world.

Antonia Laurence-Allen

18 Humorous Verse and Affectionate Parodies

Selected items from the Andrew Lang Collections of books and papers, 1860s–1910

Various formats

Provenance: acquired by gift and purchase, 20th century; also bequest of Roger Lancelyn Green, 1989

Lan PR4876.H3E87(RLG); ms30142b; first editions of 'coloured' Fairy Books

Andrew Lang (1844–1912) was both an extraordinary and a typical Victorian. A historian, classicist, anthropologist, translator, poet, novelist, literary critic and anthologist, his enthusiasms were so numerous and his output so prolific that his obituary in the *New York Times* described him as 'the most versatile man of his time in English literature'. He studied classics at the University of St Andrews, residing in St Leonard's Hall, and the earliest items by him in the library collections are contributions from the 1860s to the *St Leonard's Magazine*, a lovingly handwritten and illustrated journal in which students poke fun at subjects, including the rivalry between croquet and golf players in St Andrews and the relative shortcomings of Oxford undergraduates. Lang wrote about Oxford as 'the foreign correspondent', submitting verse on Robert Browning and other contemporary poets and 'Reasons Why They Don't Stand for the Poetry Professorship'.

Notwithstanding his youthful jibes, Lang studied at Oxford after St Andrews, remaining as a fellow until 1875, when he married and moved to London. There he became a successful journalist and produced most of the over 430 books he wrote or edited, which range from a biography of Tennyson to a reappraisal of Mary Queen of Scots, from *Myth, Ritual and Religion* (1887) – outlining theological views that Lang developed in the Gifford lectures, delivered at St Andrews – to the appealingly titled *How to Fail in Literature* (1890). He is now best remembered for his illustrated collections of fairy tales: *The Blue Fairy Book* (1889), *The Violet Fairy Book* (1901) and countless others, which delighted generations of children. Lang's interest in folk tales was rooted in the anthropological conviction that such tales were evidence of common myths shared by all cultures.

H Rider Haggard
from A. Lang.

The Andrew Lang Collections are among the richest and most diverse in the library, consisting of Lang's books (often annotated), magazines for which he wrote, lectures, manuscripts, letters and photographs. Among Lang's correspondents were Robert Louis Stevenson and H. Rider Haggard. Lang had a taste for composing humorous verses and affectionate parodies, and one of the more unusual items in the collection is *He* (1887), a parody of H. Rider Haggard's colonial adventure novel, *She*. In *He*, interestingly, the explorers who set out on a perilous journey to recover a lost mummy are female: Mary Martin, Lady Superior of Lady Betty's Hall, Oxford, and her beautiful young companion Leonora O'Dolite, Reader in English Literature on the Churton Collins Foundation. The two paddle a dhow past missile-throwing natives, fend off wild beasts, have to decipher fragmentary hieroglyphics and are betrayed by a magician. But all this occurs in the course of a trip from Oxford to London via the canal. It is far from being great literature, but it effects a fascinating transposition of the alien and the domestic, the male adventure hero and the New Woman. It is one of many items in the Lang Collections that, like Aladdin's lamp, have lain long without attracting many eyes but, when taken up afresh, offer remarkable rewards.

Sara Lodge

LONDON: LONGMANS, GREEN, & CO.

No 6.

Various Readings,

Are the result of a very corrupt state of affairs in manuscripts, of careless scribes, and of conceited editors. They are the bane of Youth, and the delight of Lushington. When is a fellow placed in a falser position, than when his text takes one reading, and his crib another, - and he gives his crib's translation of his text's reading. However so we fellows And those bumptious editors, what a row they make about nothing. Here's the way Lushy goes on, (I mean the respected Gk professional at Glasgow.) Turn over -

A selection of Andrew Lang's Fairy Books.

19 Burnished Gold and Lush, Tropical Foliage

Psalter with Sarum use calendar, *c.*1425–75

Parchment, 260 × 185mm, in modern binding
Provenance: appears in library catalogue, 1687
msBX2033.A00

From an artistic perspective, the St Andrews Psalter is the most important mediaeval manuscript held by the University of St Andrews. As such it has a prominent place in a domain of object-based teaching, also distinguished by the university's three 15th-century maces, and the architecture and sculpture of St Salvator's chapel and the cathedral priory. The manuscript contains the full text of the psalms, written in Latin in the formal 'gothic' script customarily used for religious books of its time. This is prefaced by a liturgical calendar of Sarum (Salisbury) use, and it was originally followed by the biblical hymns known as the canticles, all now cut out except part of the *Confitebor* (Isaiah 12:1–6).

Liturgical calendars, which list ecclesiastical feast days, often contain indications of the date and provenance of manuscripts, but that in the St Andrews Psalter is unhelpful on both counts. The Sarum use was followed by churches throughout much of England from the mid-13th century, and the fact that several major feasts introduced during the late Middle Ages, including the Visitation of the Blessed Virgin Mary, the Transfiguration, the Holy Name and St Osmund, are absent here suggests only that this manuscript predates *c.*1500. In any case, the style of the Psalter's artwork, which consists of eight full text-borders lavishly decorated in blue, pink, green and gold, is unmistakeably English and broadly datable between *c.*1425 and *c.*1475.

The borders occupy the positions usually chosen for significant decoration in Psalters and correspond to the division of psalm-singing in religious houses. Accordingly, there are borders at Psalms 1, 26, 38, 52, 68, 80 and 97, which were the first psalms sung at Matins on the respective days of the week, and Psalm 109, the first psalm sung at Sunday Vespers. From the burnished gold and lush, almost tropical, tangle of stylized foliage, human and animal figures occasionally emerge. Most of these, including dragons, apes, foxes, a magpie and a man in a parti-coloured jacket, are symbolically nefarious and are common in contemporary border illumination. Also common is the harping figure of the Psalms' supposed author, King David, at Psalm 1. However, the main motifs at Psalms 52 and 109 are unusual and intriguing. Psalm 52 was often illustrated with a fool, corresponding to its opening sentence: 'The fool has said in his heart: "There is no God".' Here, however, there is a figure of St Francis (identified by his grey habit, three-knotted cord and the Protestant erasure of his bleeding, stigmatized hands and feet) in 'conversation' with a magpie. The implication seems to be that the saint, and by extension his preaching-and-teaching followers, are foolish chatterboxes (the magpie symbolized idle chatter, and St Francis's famous sermon to a flock of birds was considered stupid in some circles). Psalm 109 has a yellow griffin with a scroll inscribed *Deo Gracias* in its mouth, juxtaposed with a large green parrot. A connection with the Senhouse family of Cumberland and Yorkshire, whose crest, while lacking a griffin, included a parrot with the same scroll in its beak, thus seems possible.

Although the style of the border illumination suggests manufacture in or around London and the Sarum calendar is a southern characteristic, it is perfectly possible that a fashion-conscious Senhouse commissioned it on a visit to London, the leading centre of book-manufacture in 15th-century England.

Julian Luxford

meo: et in medio multorum laudabo eum.
Qui astitit a dextris pauperis: ut salvam
faceret a persequentibus animam meam.
Dixit dominus
domino meo:
sede a dextris
meis.
Donec po
nam inimicos
tuos: scabellum
pedum tuorum.
Virgam vir
tutis tue emittet dominus ex syon: dominare
in medio inimicorum tuorum.

Confitebor tibi in seculum quia fecisti: et exspec
tabo nomen tuum quoniam bonum est in
conspectu sanctorum tuorum.
Dixit insipiens
in corde suo: non
est deus.
Corrupti sunt
et abhomina-
biles facti sunt
in iniquitatibus:
non est qui fa
ciat bonum.
Deus de celo prospexit super filios hominum:
ut videat si est intelligens aut requirens deum.

19

98

Cantate domino
canticum nouū:
quia mirabilia
fecit.
Saluauit sibi
dextera eius: et
brachiū sancṫ eius.
Notum fecit
dn̄s salutare su
um: in conspectu gentiū: reuelauit iusticiā
suam. Recordatus est misericordie sue et
ueritatis sue: domui israel.
Viderunt omnes termini terre salutare dei
nostri: iubilate deo omnis terra. cantate et
exultate et psallite.
Psallite dn̄o in cythara in cythara in uo
ce psalmi: in tubis ductilib; et uoce tube cor
nee. Iubilate in conspectu regis dn̄i: mo
ueatur mare et plenitudo eius orbis terraꝝ
et qui habitant in eo.
Flumina plaudent manu simul: montes
exultabunt a conspectu dn̄i. qm̄ uenit iudicare
terram. Iudicabit orbem terraꝝ in iusticia.
et populos in equitate.
99 Dominus regnauit irascantur ppli: qui
sedet sup cherubyn moueatur terra.

Dominus in syon magnus: et excelsus
super omnes populos.
Confiteantur nōi tuo magno qm̄ terribi
le et sc̄m est: et honor regis iudiciū diligit.
Tu parasti direcciones: iudicium et iusticia
iam in iacob tu fecisti.
Exaltate dn̄m deum nr̄m: et adorate sca
bellum pedum eius quoniam sc̄m est.
Moyses et aaron in sacerdotibus eius: et sa
muel inter eos qui invocant nomen eius.
Invocabant dn̄m et ipse exaudiebat eos:
in columpna nubis loquebatur ad eos.
Custodiebant testimonia eius: et precep
tum quod dedit illis.
Domine deus noster tu exaudiebas eos. de
us tu propicius fuisti eis: et ulciscens in omnes
adinvenciones eorum.
Exaltate dn̄m deum nr̄m: et adorate in mon
te sc̄o eius qm̄ sanctus dn̄s deus noster.
Jubilate deo om̄is terra: servite dn̄o in leticia. 100
Introite in conspectu eius: in exultacione.
Scitote qm̄ dominus ipse est deus: ipse fe
cit nos et non ipsi nos.
Populus eius et oves pascue eius introite
portas eius in confessione: atria eius in ympn
is confitemini illi.

20 Prentit at Sanct Androus

The Catechisme, that is to say, ane co[m]mone and catholik instructioun of the christin people in materis of our catholik faith and religioun … , 1552

St Andrews: [John Scot], 1552

4to, 185 × 140mm

Provenance: probably the copy listed in St Mary's College inventories of [1574] and 1598; appears in the library catalogue, 1687

Typ BS.B52SH

On first sight an unimposing volume, *The Catechisme* enjoys a special significance as the last flourishing of Catholic Scotland in print and as the first book to be printed in St Andrews. As such, it is the first book printed in Scotland outside Edinburgh. The printer, John Scot, came to St Andrews having previously worked in Edinburgh. He is not named in *The Catechisme*, but his device of Hercules and a centaur appears at the back. He evidently felt he should apologize for faults in the printing, 'committit be negligens … or be imperfection of the prent, the lettir nocht beand fullily fillit with ynk or nocht set in euin & rycht order'. This may indicate that Scot had hired inexperienced assistants for his new printing business and was frustrated with the results.

Although the work is usually known as Archbishop Hamilton's *Catechisme*, it was not written by Hamilton and is more than just a catechism: it provides a lengthy defence of the Catholic Church against its heretical critics. The book was a product of the febrile atmosphere of mid-16th-century Scotland. On the continent the Church held the Council of Trent to define more clearly its own doctrines in the wake of the Protestant Reformation that was dividing much of Europe. Against this background of increasing reformist pressure, John Hamilton, archbishop of St Andrews, summoned a series of councils of the Scottish Church with the intention of reforming the Church from within. The second of these met in St Andrews in 1552, and later that year *The Catechisme* was published. It is sometimes attributed to Richard Marshall, an English Dominican friar in exile from Edward VI's Protestant regime, but it was in fact the work of a committee of scholars and clerics assembled by Hamilton. Marshall was, in the words of historian Alec Ryrie, its 'research editor'.

The Catechisme offers detailed discussions in turn of the Commandments, the Creed, the Seven Sacraments and the Lord's Prayer, the fundamental tenets of the true faith. The doctrine throughout is orthodox, and although scholars have raised eyebrows at *The Catechisme*'s failure to defend the pope wholeheartedly or its use of scripture as the arbiter of religious doctrine, these were not indications of Protestant sympathies among the authors. Instead, the approach was deliberately ambiguous in an attempt not to exclude any of the parishioners it was trying to unite. *The Catechisme* continually reinforces Catholic teachings rather than tackling heretical ideas in a head-to-head debate.

The book was not directly aimed at laypeople. It was only to be possessed by the clergy, and it had two main aims: to improve their own religious knowledge, for 'ignorance the mother of al errours suld maist of al be eschewit in preistis', and for it to be read publicly for the instruction of parishioners every Sunday and on holy days. The order to read *The Catechisme* in church was probably widely carried out, because 16th-century Scotland had about 1,000 parishes, fewer than the average print run for a contemporary book, and few copies survive today, suggesting they were heavily used. Both copies in St Andrews University Library have been well used, and indeed one has been annotated by a reader.

The Catholic reform movement of which *The Catechisme* was a centrepiece was ultimately overtaken by the Scottish Reformation in 1559–60, but the book itself stands as a monument to the reforming efforts of Archbishop Hamilton and as a window into the religious culture destroyed by the Reformation.

John McCallum

ur declaratioun of the ten commandis, geuin to vs be almychty God, to quhome be geuin al louing and thankis, honour and glore for euir and euer. Amen.

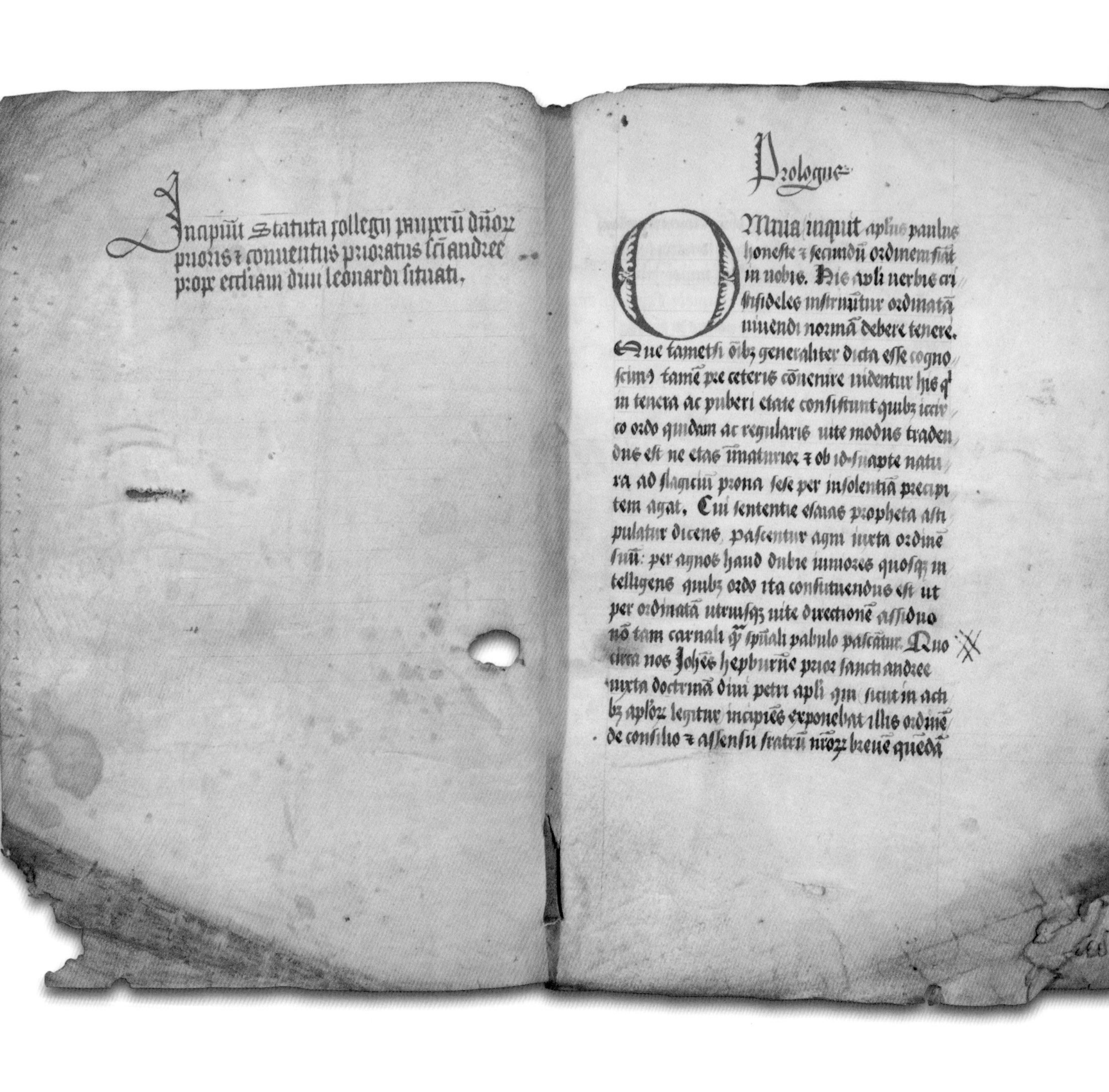

Incipiūt statuta collegii pauperū dñoꝝ
prioris ꝛ conventus prioratus sci andree
prope ecclesiam divi leonardi situati.

Prologus

Omnia inquit aplus paulus
honeste ꝛ secundū ordinem fiāt
in nobis. His apli verbis cri
stifideles instruūtur ordinatā
vivendi normā debere tenere.
Que tametsi oībꝫ generaliter dicta esse cogno
scimꝰ tamē pre ceteris convenire videntur his q
in tenera ac puberi etate consistunt quibꝫ idcir
co ordo quidam ac regularis vite modus traden
dus est ne etas immaturior ꝛ ob id suapte natu
ra ad flagitiū prona sese per insolentiā precipi
tem agat. Cui sententie esaias propheta asti
pulatur dicens, pascentur agni iuxta ordinē
suū: per agnos haud dubie iuniores quosque in
telligens quibꝫ ordo ita constituendus est ut
per ordinatā utriusque vite directionē assiduo
nō tam carnali q̄ spūali pabulo pascātur. Quo
circa nos Johēs hepburnē prior sancti andree
iuxta doctrinā divi petri apli qui sicut in acti
bꝫ aploꝝ legitur incipiēs exponebat illis ordinē
de consilio ꝛ assensu fratrū nroꝝ breve quedā

21 Free from the Approaches of Women

Statutes of St Leonard's College, 1544

Parchment, 240 × 170mm with pendant seal, in modern binding
Provenance: created for the college
UYSL165/2

The College of St Leonard was founded in 1512 as a 'college of poor clerks' by Alexander Stewart, archbishop-designate of St Andrews (illegitimate son of King James IV) and John Hepburn, prior of St Andrews. Hepburn appears to have been the moving force in this endowment, adapting for the purpose the ancient hospital adjoining the church of St Leonard within the northwest corner of the priory precinct, in an attempt to improve clerical education particularly within the Augustinian order. Stewart, who had been educated on the continent under Erasmus, was an enthusiastic proponent of the new learning that encompassed humanist ideals, but Hepburn sought a return to the discipline of monastic values. Stewart's support secured crown confirmation of the foundation by James IV on 23 February 1513, but there was no papal bull confirming rights and privilege, perhaps because of the death of the young archbishop at the battle of Flodden in September 1513.

The original statutes of St Leonard's College (now lost) concerned admission, the conduct of divine service, student discipline, appointments and administrative matters. Students were to be no younger than 15 and no older than 21 to gain admission to St Leonard's College – although students as young as 12 were able to enter the Faculty of Arts at this time. The statutes drawn up in 1544 represent a revision of the originals in an effort to tighten observance and discipline, and they reflect the tension between traditional and new learning as mirrored in the different emphases of the two founders, as well as a reaction to the turbulent religious events of the time.

The Latin statutes are written on 14 folios in eight sections with headings in red ink. The document is now bound between boards with marbled endpapers but still bears one of the two seals with which it was authenticated, those of the cathedral chapter (missing) and the college. Approval of this attempt to bring order to the institution is indicated through the subscription of the signatures of Subprior John Winram, Canon John Annand of St Andrews as principal of the college, Thomas Fyff as sacristan, John Lawmonth as provisor and James Wylke, David Guild, John Scheyll and David Gardyne as regents. The ratification by James Stewart, commendator of the priory, and Alexander Mylne, abbot of Cambuskenneth (his administrator), is dated 8 September 1544.

The minutiae of college life are ordered by the statutes, including precise measures of food and drink allowed at particular times. They also list chores to be performed by the students, such as 'clearing spiders' webs and other filth' before Christmas and Easter, the requirement to wear gowns and hoods when outside the college and 'not to hold feastings at night, wear knives or weapons of offence within the walls, play dice at all, or football, or any other dishonest or dangerous games'. Contemporary monastic prejudice is demonstrated in the ruling that no woman may set foot in the college 'save the common laundress, who must be fifty years at the least, because, saith Hieronymus, he cannot abide with God with his whole heart who is not free from the approaches of women'.

'Statutes' might be thought to bear the connotation of dull administrative record, but this startling example demonstrates how the university's rich collegiate archives can illuminate for us the personal and institutional lives of our academic ancestors.

Christine McGladdery

22 'Yet have I Words that are Sweeter'

Bustan of Sa'di, late 18th century

Paper, 2,850 × 90mm

Provenance: gift of Robert Dundas, 2nd viscount Melville and chancellor of the University, 1847

ms31(O)

The *Bustan*, or *Orchard*, is a Persian epic poem written in the 13th century by Sheikh Mosleh al-Din Sa'di Shirazi. This copy of the poem is presented in a highly unusual, possibly unique, form on a long, narrow roll of very fine, almost translucent paper, written in black with red highlights and lavishly bordered in gold. When the *Bustan* is exhibited it immediately draws attention, because of the marked contrast it presents to the books, codices and letters that normally surround it. Not only does its striking physical appearance – its form, the intricate pattern and the extravagant use of gold – catch the eye, but there is often a visible reaction at the moment of realization that the leaves and highly stylized Persian script are composed of tiny writing, the text of the poem.

The scroll starts with a dedication, written in gold in highly flattering language, to King George III, 'King of Great Britain, France and Ireland'. The title *Bustan* is then followed by a pattern of rose leaves comprising the minute text of the poem, interspersed with four sections in which the minuscule writing repeats the dedication. The whole is bordered with a small foliate design in gold, with elaborate ends to the border. The work is not dated, and at the foot is a name, Mir 'Ali Amjad Khan, who is presumed to have been the calligrapher.

A letter dated April 1790 from Sir Charles W. Rouse Boughton, secretary of the Board of Control of India, to Henry Dundas, later 1st viscount Melville, describes the roll in detail. The author is of the opinion that the whole of the poem, some 8,000 lines, is worked into the pattern. He concludes: 'The writing is very elegant and in general correct, but hardly legible, without the help of glasses!'

Sa'di was born in Shiraz, where his father held a position of distinction at court and his maternal uncle was a celebrated cleric. He studied Arabic literature and Sufi mysticism in Baghdad, then spent many years travelling throughout the Middle East and Central Asia. Returning home to Shiraz, he composed the works for which he is known today, 24 named works collected together within 30 years of his death. Sa'di is still regarded with great affection in contemporary Iran, and his writings are widely known and quoted. His moral anecdotes often use humour to deliver serious Sufi messages about life and worldliness.

The *Bustan* was inspired by his travels. The poem consists of ten themed chapters containing moral stories, prayers and aphorisms on love, justice, gratitude, repentance and humility, gathered during his years of wandering. He says, 'I reaped advantages in every corner, and gleaned an ear of corn from every harvest' and 'I regretted that I should go from the garden of the world empty-handed to my friends', and reflected: 'Travellers bring sugar-candy from Egypt as a present to their friends. Although I have no candy, yet have I words that are sweeter. The sugar that I bring is not that which is eaten, but what knowers of truth take away with respect.'

It is fitting that Sa'di's gift to his friends is encapsulated in this beautiful manuscript, whose magnificence inspires wonder in those who look on it.

Moira Mackenzie

فدوی نمک پروردہ میر علی امجد خان قاضی سرکار ایلور

Actual size.

23 A World Teeming with Detail

Sebastian Münster, *Cosmographiae universalis lib[ri] VI*, 1550

Basel: Heinrich Petri, 1550
Folio, 328 × 205mm
Provenance: gift of Lord James Stewart to St Leonard's College, 1550s or 1560s
Roy G96.M8B50

For its ability to elicit wonder while imparting knowledge Münster's *Cosmographia* was acclaimed in the 16th century and is no less treasured now. It represented the culmination of 20 years of work for the Professor of Hebrew at the University of Basel. Its compass and ambition were remarkable, and the erudition and energy its completion required were breathtaking.

In an early reflection on his task, Münster wrote that the art of cosmography records and concerns itself with: 'the countries, habitations and lives of the various peoples of the earth, but also with many other things, such as strange animals, trees, metals … the habits, customs, laws and governments of men … the origins of countries, regions, cities and towns, how nature has endowed them and what human inventiveness has produced in them, [also] such notable things as have happened everywhere.'

At once a scholarly geography of the entire world and all its history, an encyclopedia, a travel guide and a catalogue of the wonders wrought by nature and by man, lavishly and vividly illustrated throughout, Münster's cosmography was a huge success, an early modern bestseller. It would eventually see 35 editions between 1544 and 1628, and it was translated into five languages, endlessly excerpted, copied, referenced and imitated. This Latin edition of 1550 was the definitive version produced during Münster's own lifetime, and this copy, one of two in the library's collections, was given to St Leonard's College by former student Lord James Stewart, later the regent Moray.

The *Cosmographia* was the first work of geography to depict the then-known continents with separate maps and the first to offer a separate map of England. It presented the earliest map of Africa available and the oldest woodcut of Scandinavia obtainable. Its 'cut-away' mining diagrams and maps depicting contemporary religious allegiances were likewise precocious innovations. The method by which the information about the regions and cities of Europe was collected is of striking significance. Münster cultivated a pan-European network of like-minded enthusiasts who recorded cartographical data, pored over local records and commissioned proud representations of their cities, sending the fruits of their toil to Münster, in wholehearted support of his project and so that their native lands should be accurately depicted and rightly celebrated. It is this tone of celebration and wonder that defines the contents of the *Cosmographia*. In a period of escalating religious conflict, it was made possible by an ongoing harmony of spirit among the learned, and it represents a chronicle of the shared interests, tastes and enthusiasms of the broad literate public.

Finely poised between empirical research and lively anecdote, between the intellectual cultures of the mediaeval and the modern scholar, the *Cosmographia* throws open countless windows to every aspect of the early modern world. In so doing, Münster invited his contemporaries to regard themselves and their neighbours and to consider their present good fortune in a cosmos in which ceaseless change remained the only constant. Through this book those windows remain open for us to look through at a world teeming with detail, centuries-distant but strikingly familiar.

Matthew McLean

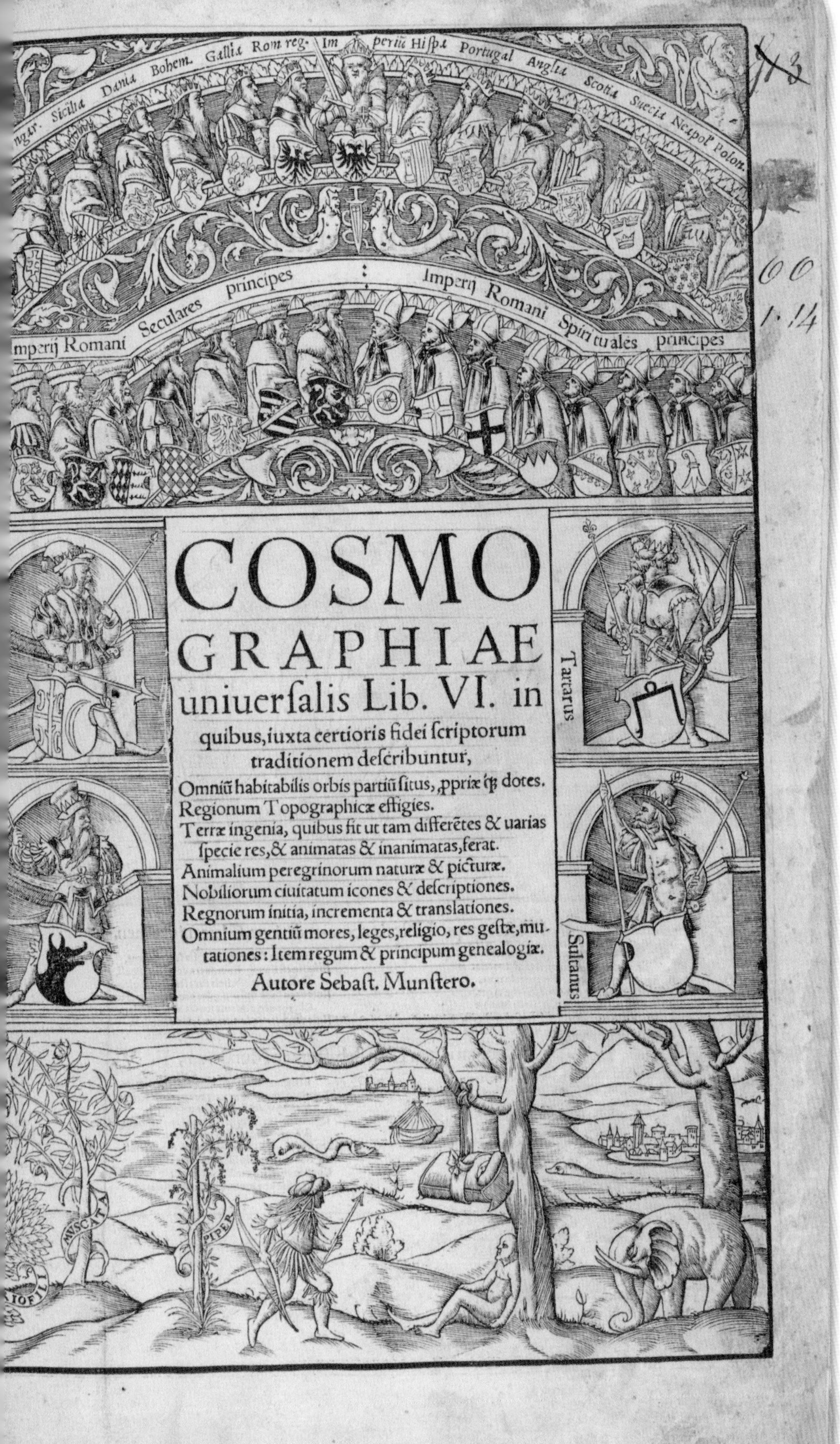

COSMOGRAPHIAE

universalis Lib. VI. in quibus, iuxta certioris fidei scriptorum traditionem describuntur,

Omniũ habitabilis orbis partiũ situs, ꝓpriæq́ꝫ dotes.
Regionum Topographicæ effigies.
Terræ ingenia, quibus fit ut tam differẽtes & uarias specie res, & animatas & inanimatas, ferat.
Animalium peregrinorum naturæ & picturæ.
Nobiliorum ciuitatum icones & descriptiones.
Regnorum initia, incrementa & translationes.
Omnium gentiũ mores, leges, religio, res gestæ, mutationes: Item regum & principum genealogiæ.

Autore Sebast. Munstero.

Rubeaquum cum arce Isenburgo moen

e ætatis habitudinem ad uiuum expressum.

24 The Arts of War

Portfolio of drawings by Mutio Oddi of Urbino and others, 17th century

Paper, various-sized sheets folded to 350 × 240mm, loosely bound in card
Provenance: purchased with generous financial assistance from the National Fund for Acquisitions, 2008
ms38654

The profession of architect-engineer at the turn of the 16th century was a diverse one. As masters of fortifications and the arts of war in general, architect-engineers were obliged to obtain expertise in arithmetic and geometry, surveying, mechanics and drawing (in both plan and perspective), so that they might design and construct fortifications correctly and explain their ideas to officers. In Italy, in particular, military engineering advanced at a rapid pace, thanks especially to the development there of the so-called *trace Italienne*, a new form of fortification based on the angled bastion. By *c.*1600, however, Italian expertise had spread (thanks in no small part to the mobility of engineers, who necessarily travelled to where conflicts were actually taking place) across Europe, notably to the Netherlands, which had been riven by war with Spain.

Both the range of skills demanded of architect-engineers and the international nature of the profession are encapsulated in the rare album of text and images acquired by the library in 2008. A collection of sheets in various hands, the album runs to some 158 pages, most of which (on the basis of watermarks) may be dated to the first few decades of the 17th century and which seem to have been made by Italian and Spanish individuals familiar with the arts of war in both southern and northern Europe. The album comprises notes on geometry, designs for fortifications, annotated drawings recording European forts and famous sieges (such as Asti and Grave in the Netherlands), and sketches of buildings, including Roman churches and the famous circular staircase at the Cortile del Belvedere in the Vatican. At least four different hands are discernible in the album, but the only one to whom a name may be given at present is the Italian polymath Mutio Oddi of Urbino (1569–1639), whose signed and dated letter of 1633 – concerned with the construction of a new lighthouse at Pesaro, in the Duchy of Urbino – appears at pages 116–20.

Oddi, a famous mathematician and instrumentalist, had been the duke of Urbino's personal architect before his supposed involvement in a coup to overthrow his lord resulted in a prison sentence and eventual exile from his homeland. He spent most of the rest of his life in Milan and, latterly, Lucca, where he was appointed chief fortifications engineer to the republic, completing a major part of Lucca's defences. We know from Oddi's surviving letters that he owned a plan of the fort of Fuentes, an example of which is in the St Andrews album (pages 2–3), and it seems likely that some of the album's sheets were once in his possession. Notably, Oddi had many pupils in mathematics and the military arts, including the engineers Giuseppe Barca and Giovanni Battista Caravaggio. The St Andrews album may well have been compiled by one of Oddi's students as a working set of drawings and notes – a sort of 'aide-memoire' that was easily portable and that could be added to as the engineer travelled across the continent.

Intriguingly, the album seems to be connected to the early modern literature on warfare, for the careful drawing of the siege of Grave (page 149) appears to have been the model for the engraved plate (cut by the Antwerp engraver Joachim Trognaesius) in Pompeo Giustiniani's *Della Guerre di Fiandra* (Antwerp, 1609). One wonders if part of the album might have been formed by Giustiniani (1555–1624), a celebrated *Maestro di Campo* who saw service in the Netherlands.

The album is thus an extremely valuable record of the working habits of an early modern military professional. Situated between science and art, it reminds us that the arts of war were a dynamic, changeable set of practices of international scope. Much remains to be discovered about the fortunes of the album, its compiler and authors: it is a treasure that demands further study.

Alexander Marr

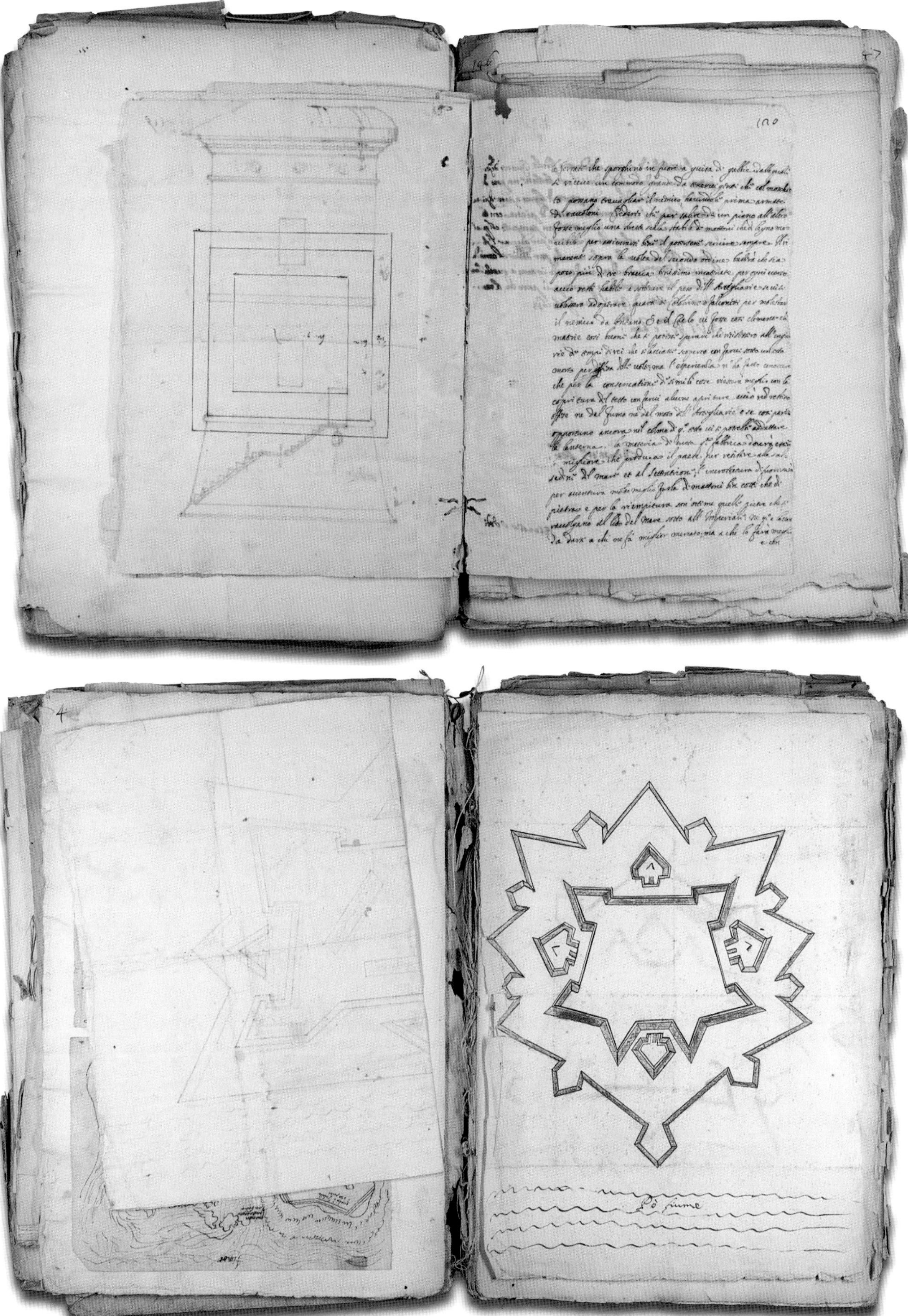
Pò fiume

P A L V D
B
D
H
B
D
H
I
D
B
G
G
G
I
A

A
B
B
B
A
A
GRAVE
A
A
A

This Book Was Begone at sea the 10 of aprill anno 1662
being com from ams[illegible] for the Ellie
Where I live [illegible] countie of fyfe

Wreatine By
Alexander Gillespie with my
Hand the 13 of aprill anno 1662

to Gods Glorie And our conforte

Upon the 2 of desember 1662
I Was contracted with [illegible] small
Upon the 30 of januarie 1663 We
Was mairied by Mr Robert Weimis he being
minister of [illegible] at that tyme being friday
of ye Weeke

Alexander Gillespie Wreatene With my hand
at the kowes road the 11th of november
anno domini 1663

AG

25 Ransomed for a Hogshead of Beer

Seafaring journal of Alexander Gillespie, 1662–85

Paper, folded to 205 × 306mm and stitched
Provenance: gift of Sir Alexander Sharp Bethune, 1997
ms38352

Gillespie's journal is a very rare survival, kindly donated to the library by a direct descendant. Most of our knowledge of trade in this period comes from administrative documents, such as customs records, and a few personal letters. This private volume systematically chronicles the main years in the career of Alexander Gillespie, born in 1635, the son of a Fife skipper from Elie. He would also have kept account books and a ship's log (the library holds a rare example, two pages of the log of the *George* of Pittenweem, on a voyage from Crail to Stockholm in 1689). Gillespie, however, records a personal account of his journeys and the problems he encountered. It is consciously written in English, not Scots, though there are occasional lapses. His narrative style is crisp and brief. At the back, and occasionally among the main text, are navigational aide-memoires.

The journal is simply made, of sheets of paper folded, cut and sewn. It starts on 10 April 1662 and records his marriage on 30 January 1663 to Christian Small, the daughter of an Elie skipper. Inside the front cover he notes the births of seven children. To work independently, a merchant skipper needed not only seamanship but also a trusted partner ashore (usually a spouse) to keep accounts and deal with potential suppliers and customers. The journal records the sending of 21 letters, almost all to 'hom'.

The volume covers 23 years, to 31 July 1685. During this time there were national and international events that affected where Gillespie went and what cargoes he carried. There were wars with the Dutch in 1665–7 and 1672–4. During the war between France and Holland (1674–8) Gillespie had six encounters with privateers between Dover and Ushant who demanded a ransom, such as a hogshead of beer or £5 scots per person.

One interesting feature that emerges is how little time he actually spent at sea. After loading a cargo somewhere in the Firth of Forth, he would travel along the coast to await the right wind for safe open-sea crossing to Norway, the Baltic, Holland or from the south coast of England to western France. On arrival he would have to wait for quayside space before unloading, which took several days. Then he would negotiate a return cargo and lie at anchor until conditions were right for the return journey. In round figures he appears to have spent 30 per cent of his time in port, 30 per cent at home and 40 per cent at sea, but of that, 45 per cent was at anchor, 45 per cent coasting, and only 10 per cent crossing the open waters.

Gillespie made good profits from an average of just under three voyages a year. In 1676 he got a lift with another skipper to Rotterdam, and spent six months supervising the building of his new, larger ship, the *James*. With this he concentrated on the run to Bordeaux to bring the new vintage home in time for Hogmanay. In 1682 he and Christian built a fine new house in South Street, Elie, the doorpiece of which survives. Christian inherited half the estate of Wester Newton Reres in the parish of Kilconquhar, and in 1677 Gillespie was able to buy the other half. His heirs were landed gentry and never went to sea again.

Paula Martin

26 The Most Celebrated Scottish Intellectual of the Renaissance

Andrew Melville's copy of George Buchanan, *Rerum Scoticarum Historia*, 1582

Edinburgh: Alexander Arbuthnet, 1582

Folio, 290 × 195mm

Provenance: ownership inscriptions of Andrew Melville, William Scott and Edward Wright, 1750; immediate source of acquisition unknown

Buch DA775.B8B82

Among the most important collections of rare books in the library are the 260 volumes by or about George Buchanan (1506–82), the most celebrated Scottish intellectual of the Renaissance. A graduate of St Andrews and for a time principal of St Leonard's College, Buchanan was at the cutting edge of the 16th-century revival of classical learning. Revered by contemporaries as 'the prince of poets', his Latin verse was thought to rival and even surpass that of his Roman models, and the many editions of his poetry in the library's Buchanan Collection testify to the high esteem in which he was held in the learned culture of early modern Europe.

Today, however, Buchanan is remembered less for his poetry than for his political polemics. In his later years he turned his literary gifts to partisan ends, justifying the overthrow of his former patron, Mary Queen of Scots, in 1567 and popularizing an image of her as a murderous adulterer that still affronts Mary's legions of admirers. A key text in this smear campaign was a massive history

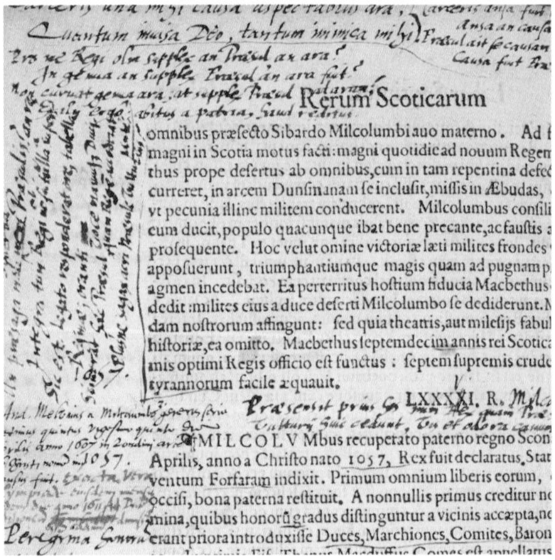

Rerum Scoticarum

omnibus præfecto Sibardo Milcolumbi auo materno. Ad
magni in Scotia motus facti: magni quotidie ad nouum Regem
thus prope desertus ab omnibus, cum in tam repentina defec
curreret, in arcem Dunsinanam se inclusit, missis in Æbudas,
vt pecunia illinc militem conducerent. Milcolumbus consili
cum ducit, populo quacunque ibat bene precante, ac faustis
prosequente. Hoc velut omine victoriæ læti milites frondes
apposuerunt, triumphantiumque magis quam ad pugnam p
agmen incedebat. Ea perterritus hostium fiducia Macbethus
dedit: milites eius a duce deserti Milcolumbo se dediderunt. M
dam nostrorum affingunt: sed quia theatris, aut milesijs fabul
historiæ, ea omitto. Macbethus septemdecim annis rei Scotic
anis optimi Regis officio est functus: septem supremis crude
tyrannorum facile æquauit.

LXXXXI. R.

MILCOLVMbus recuperato paterno regno Scon
Aprilis, anno a Christo nato 1057, Rex fuit declaratus. Stat
ventum Forfaram indixit. Primum omnium liberis eorum,
occisi, bona paterna restituit. A nonnullis primus creditur n
mina, quibus honorũ gradus distinguntur a vicinis accæpta, n
erant priora introduxisse Duces, Marchiones, Comites, Baron

of Scotland, *Rerum Scoticarum Historia*, written in the last decade of his life when the queen was in an English prison and Buchanan was employed as tutor to her son, James VI. The *Historia* was published in 1582, the year of its author's death, by the Edinburgh printer Alexander Arbuthnet. This copy of the first edition is uniquely important because it was owned by Buchanan's young friend and disciple, Andrew Melville (1545–1622), and is extensively annotated in his hand.

Melville is best known as an outspoken defender of Presbyterianism, a Church free from royal interference and control. He was also, like Buchanan, a brilliant classical scholar, steeped in the languages and literature of the ancient world. His intellectual prowess was recognized by his appointment as principal of St Mary's College in the University of St Andrews in 1580, aged barely 35. He held the post for 25 years until King James (from 1603 king of England as well as of Scotland) ran out of patience with his most irascible clerical critic, imprisoning him in the Tower of London in 1606 and exiling him to France in 1611.

Among the books Melville had with him in the Tower was his copy of Buchanan's *Historia*. In fact, the extensive marginalia, all in Latin and of varying legibility, suggest several readings of the text, of which at least one was in the Tower. Such biographical snippets are useful for historians, but the real importance of the marginalia lies in the insights they provide into how Melville responded to Buchanan's views on such matters as the antiquity of the Scottish kingdom, the history of Christianity in Scotland and the legitimacy of Mary's deposition. Whether simply noting Buchanan's words, almost always with approval, or responding more fully – sometimes in the form of original Latin poems – Melville's marginalia add immeasurable value to Buchanan's book and ensure its prominent place among the library's many treasures.

Roger Mason

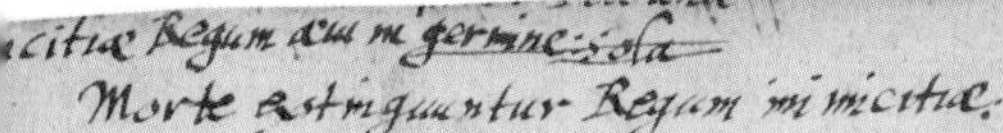

RERVM SCOTICARVM HISTORIA

AVCTORE

Georgio Buchanano

Scoto.

EDIMBVRGI

Apud Alexandrum Arbuthnetum Typographum Regium

Anno M. D. LXXXII.

CVM PRIVILEGIO REGALI.

Edward Wright. Edinburg. Empt. die 9no Aug. A.D. 1750

27 Hunting the Green Lion

Three manuscripts by Isaac Newton, *c.*1700

Paper, (a) 305 × 186mm, (b) 184 × 293mm, (c) 307 × 186mm
Provenance: purchased for the university by John Read, Professor of Chemistry (1923–63); transferred to the custody of the library, 1989
ms38195(a), (b), (c) – depicted

Sir Isaac Newton's preoccupation with alchemy and alchemical experimentation in addition to his other esoteric interests is now well known, although 18th- and 19th-century commentators did their best to conceal this extensive part of his legacy by consigning to obscurity those packets of alchemical, theological and chronological material they described as 'of very little interest in themselves'. Newton, however, was perfectly serious about this work, and one of his assistants recorded how 'he used to employ about six weeks [at a time] in his laboratory, the fire scarcely going out either day or night … till he had finished his alchemical experiments'. He was not trying to produce gold but to show that the operations of nature, as demonstrated in alchemy, might provide evidence for God's active presence in the universe. His alchemy thus sprang from his religious convictions.

Newton's alchemical manuscripts can be found in several places, the majority in the Keynes Collection at King's College, Cambridge, and others in the United States, Switzerland and Israel. St Andrews has three in Newton's own hand. One (c) contains a list of alchemists' names – Hermes (Trismegistus), Maria (the Jewess), Raimund Lull, John Dee and so forth – with the titles of alchemical works including *Clangor Buccinae*, *Scala Philosophorum*, *Rosarium Magnum* and *Splendor Solis*, and the *Aurora Consurgens* attributed to St Thomas Aquinas.

A second (a), entitled 'The hunting of the green lion', is a single sheet with writing on both sides. The language is English and describes a distillation process in 15 stages. At several points in the description, Newton adds amendments or qualifications above the line – for example, 'a copious black excrement which will subside' becomes 'a copious black, impure, gritty precipitate or sediment or excrement'. The whole is a mixture of immediately comprehensible instructions or observations and alchemical shorthand or jargon in the form of imagery, of which the 'green lion' of the title is an example. This is entirely within the usual tradition of alchemical writing. The alchemist would look for colour changes marking each stage of his experiment, each colour often symbolized by an animal. The 'green lion' could be the green tinge produced by the action of acid on metal, or chlorophyll from the decomposition of vegetable matter.

The third manuscript (b) consists of a single sheet written on one side in Latin. It is the record of an experiment in six stages and begins, as one might expect, with distillation. Burning, further distillation, decoction for 30 days, calcination and sublimation follow, with Newton observing the rising and falling of lighter and heavier substances or liquids until he comes to the final stage. 'Note,' he writes, 'that the green lion causes the black body to evaporate along with the destruction of its form. It is a dirty substance, so it must be prepared so that anything foreign to it is separated from it. Let it be distilled on its own. First of all an acidic water rises during the procedure, like natural vinegar, only more spiritual. Then a white oil rises, which will float on top of the water. Then rise a white smoke and a spirit and an oil tending to a yellowish colour which afterwards becomes red like blood. It is extremely penetrating and smells very bad.'

While containing nothing out of the alchemical ordinary, these manuscripts reflect very well that intense toil and meticulous note-taking and observation that Newton brought to his work in the laboratory over his many years as a Fellow of Trinity College, Cambridge.

P.G. Maxwell-Stuart

Itali

Morienus
Tho. Aquinas
Petrus Bonus Ferrariensis
Petrus de Zalento
Augurellus
Marcellus Palingenius
Joannes de Rupescissa
Augustinus Pantheus
Aloysius Marlianus
Janus Lacinius
Ferrarius Mon.
Vide Symb. aur. p 587, 588.
Laurentius Ventura Venetus

Hispani

Raymundus Lullius

Galli

Arnoldus. Flamellus. Chr: Parisiensis
Joannes Fernelius. Bern: Trevirensis
Gulielmus Parisiensis. Dionys. Zacharius
Gratianus. Ægidius de Vadis. D'Espagnet.
Vincentius Bellnacensis. Joan: de Meheung. Guido de Montanor. Tauladan. Joan. Palmarius.
David Lagneus. Nuisement. Faber. Mundanus.

Germani

Albertus Magnus. Isaac Hollandus
Joannes Pontanus. Lambspring
Joannes de Padua. Basil. Valentinus
Author Rosarij magni. Alanus
Author dialogi inter aurum & lapidem
Jodocus Greverus. Joan: Willichius. Paracelsus.
Ulstadius. Grassaeus. Maierus.

Sarmatae

Joannes Zetzinensis. Bohemus
Joannes de Laznioro Bohemus
Wenceslaus Lavinius Moravus
Mich. Sendivogius Polonus
Nicholaus Melchior Cibinensis Transylvanus

Angli

Rasis Cestrensis.
Merlinus.
Richardus Anglus
Rogerius Bacon
Robertus Vallensis
Dunstanus Archiep. Cant.
Geo Ripleius
Joannes Dumbelius
Joannes Belye
Joan. Daustenius
Tho. Nortonus
Sam. Nortonus
Joan. Dee. Edw. Kelley
Tho Rawlin.
Philaletha.
Hortulanus.

28 Property of the Highest Quality?

Gilbert Francklyn, *Observations, occasioned by the attempts made in England to effect the abolition of the slave trade*, 1788

Kingston, Jamaica: Thomas Strupar and Joseph Preston, 1788
8vo, 228 × 144mm
Provenance: ownership inscription of Sir George Strickland; purchased 2009
r HT1098.O3 (SR)

This very rare item was purchased by the library in 2009; only two other libraries in the world are known to have copies. It is the 1788 first edition of a pamphlet later attributed to Gilbert Francklyn, a veteran of the sugar estates of the West Indies. His object is to offer 'an exact account of the common and usual treatment of slaves' in response to the 'calumnies' broadcast by Thomas Clarkson's Committee against slavery, which had met for the first time at James Phillips's bookstore and printworks in London on 22 May 1787.

In the certainty that slavery is both natural and sanctioned by the scriptures, Francklyn stoutly refutes accusations of cruelty on the part of 'West Indian gentlemen': while the lower class of overseer may occasionally act viciously, a slave owner would no sooner impair the worth of a slave through ill-treatment than a sensible English farmer would risk devaluing his horses in the same way. On the contrary, Francklyn asserts, slaves are generously provided with housing, food, clothes and medical treatment. 'Breeding women', he notes, are treated with particular delicacy.

Today's reader will experience scepticism and distaste at Francklyn's description of the 'abundance of ... goats, kids, and hogs ... turkeys, capons, Guinea fowls ... hams, tongues, and fish of different kinds ... plenty of rum at least, and not unfrequently wine and porter' enjoyed by slaves. Likewise his claims that 'flagellations are inflicted with so much care, as rarely to disable the offender from work' or that sick slaves have sometimes to be detained in the stocks, lest they further injure their health by attending an insalubrious 'negro dance'. Perhaps Francklyn's political arguments command more understanding when he observes that almost nobody in contemporary society enjoyed real freedom and certainly not the distressed poor of England. He suggests that Europeans should look first to their own laws and customs before interfering in West Indian ones. Although Francklyn claims no philosophical pretensions, these questions of self-government and individual liberty reflect the preoccupations of a year poised between the adoption of the Constitution in the United States (1787) and the outbreak of the French Revolution (1789).

But the most remarkable aspect of this item is undoubtedly the object itself. For these very pages, extolling the benefits of slavery, were almost certainly printed by slaves. By the 1780s Jamaica had several thriving print shops, producing newspapers, gazettes, tickets and handbills, including notices of slave auctions. Several of those businesses owned slaves, and among them were Strupar & Preston of Harbour Street, Kingston, which produced Francklyn's work.

If, according to Francklyn, 'it is well known, that from 70 to 80 pounds sterling, is the common value of an able, seasoned, field negro' while an expert tradesman 'may be worth from 100 to 500 pounds sterling', we might surmise that Chelsea (valued at £20) and Tom (£90), both inventoried some years later as pressmen owned by the printer Thomas Strupar, were not viewed as property of the highest quality. How they in turn viewed their own existence we can only imagine. And nor do we know whether they lived to see the abolition of the slave trade in 1807, the result of a 20-year campaign begun one May evening in another, distant print shop of London's Old Jewry.

Lorna Milne

Sir Geo Strickland Bart.
Yorkshire

OBSERVATIONS,

Occasioned by the attempts made in ENGLAND to effect the Abolition

OF THE

SLAVE TRADE;

SHEWING

The manner in which NEGROES are treated in the BRITISH COLONIES

IN THE

WEST INDIES;

AND, ALSO,

Some particular *REMARKS* on a *LETTER* addressed to the *Treasurer* of the *Society* for effecting such *Abolition*,

FROM THE

Reverend Mr. ROBERT BOUCHER NICHOLLS,

DEAN of MIDDLEHAM.

" And why beholdest thou the mote that is in thy brother's eye, but considerest not the beam that is in thine own eye?"

" Or how wilt thou say to thy brother, let me pull out the mote out of thine eye; and behold, a beam is in thine own eye?"

KINGSTON, JAMAICA:

PRINTED BY

THOMAS STRUPAR AND JOSEPH PRESTON,

IN HARBOUR-STREET.

M,DCC,LXXXVIII.

29 Truly, a Remarkable Man

D'Arcy Wentworth Thompson's annotated copy of *On Growth and Form*, 1942

4to, 1 vol. bound in 2, interleaved and annotated, 207 × 137mm
Provenance: from the papers of D'Arcy Wentworth Thompson, bequeathed 1948
ms42363-4

D'Arcy Wentworth Thompson was a polymath of a sort that one simply never encounters today. Equally qualified to occupy chairs in zoology, mathematics and classics, his writings encompassed all these fields, as exemplified by his *Glossary of Greek Birds* (1895), *Science and the Classics* (1940) and *Glossary of Greek Fishes* (1947). However, the work for which he is best remembered and honoured is *On Growth and Form*, first published in 1917, with a second edition in 1942 and an abridged edition edited by John Tyler Bonner in 1961. It has been translated into many languages and is still in print.

In this elegantly written book, he advanced his main thesis: that biological form can reflect physical and mathematical principles. One clear demonstration of his notions of the dynamic influence of starting conditions lies in the morphology of shells and horns. These are the permanent, non-living, three-dimensional record of a temporary, two-dimensional living state – the base of the horn or the mantle of the shellfish. D'Arcy Thompson showed that all horn and shell morphologies could be described in simple mathematical terms readily derived from the incremental nature of growth.

Perhaps the most famous images from *On Growth and Form* are the transformations. D'Arcy showed that gross variation in form between related species could be modelled by the consistent deformation of a sheet, and that if the sheet were stretched in one particular pattern, a new species form would be generated. His work still has relevance for mathematical, evolutionary and developmental biologies and for the interface between science and the arts. He focused on the boundaries between disciplines in a remarkably modern manner.

D'Arcy was born in 1860 and was appointed to the Chair of Biology at Dundee in 1884. He moved to St Andrews in 1917, and died, still occupying the Chair of Natural History, in 1948. He was a great character, whose memory was cherished by students and townsfolk alike. He loved wine, women and song – 'I must dance just once more before I die', was a favourite saying of his. An honours student was once summoned over poor work. She had been to a party the night before and was surprised to be greeted with, 'was it a good dance?' She replied that it was. Then, 'is it a good floor?' and lastly, 'got a boy of your own?' He loved children and always had time for them. A correspondent recalled visiting the Bell Pettigrew Museum of Natural History (which D'Arcy ran) in 1932 when he was a boy of eight. He was hailed by the professor, who showed him round the exhibits and on parting gave him a jar of stick insects, with instructions to feed them on fresh privet leaves.

The winter before he died D'Arcy was teaching the history of natural history to a group of students at his home. One day as he read aloud he seemed to be hesitating, and one of the girls, fearing that he was unwell, said, 'Are you tired, Professor, should we go now?' D'Arcy replied, 'My dear child, I am not tired. I happen to be reading you a piece of mediaeval Italian, and I find the translation a little difficult.' Truly, he was a remarkable man.

Martin Milner

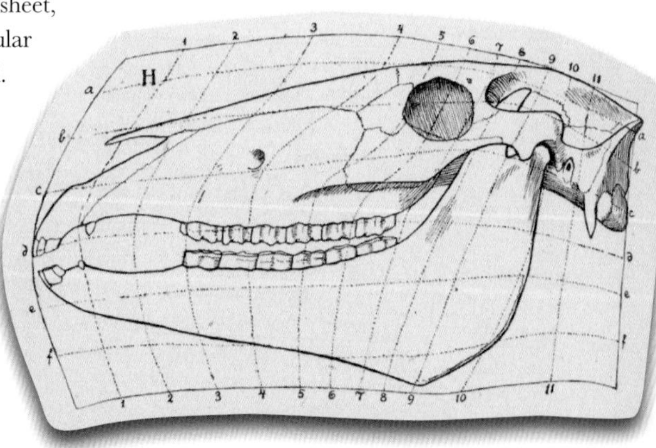

this series with the figure of *Polyprion*, in Fig. 521, we see that outlines of *Pseudopriacanthus* (Fig. 522) and of *Sebastes* or *paena* (Fig. 523) are easily derived by substituting a system

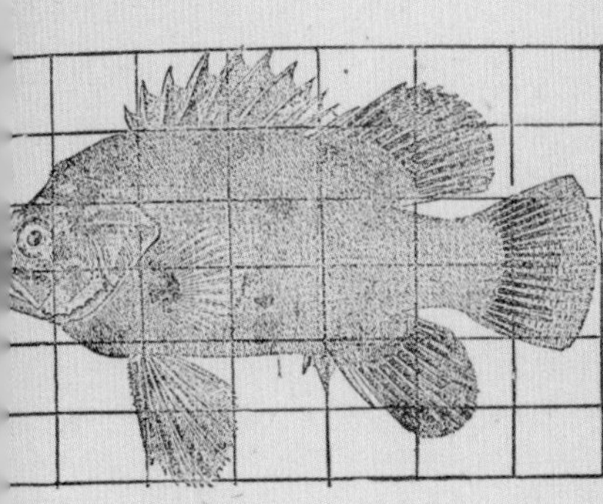

Fig. 521. *Polyprion.*

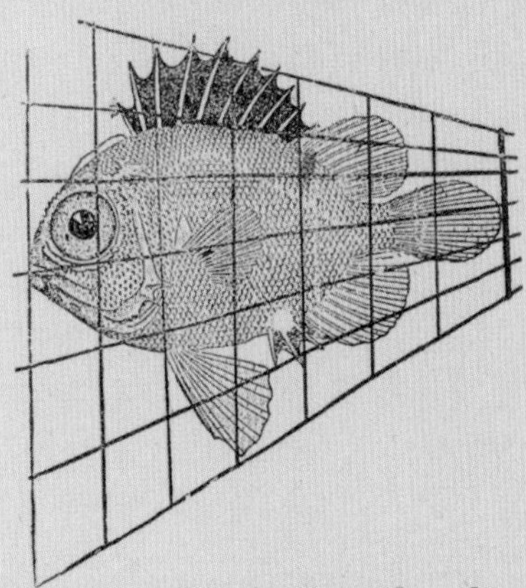

Fig. 522. *Pseudopriacanthus altus.*

riangular, or radial, coordinates for the rectangular ones in which had inscribed *Polyprion*. The very curious fish *Antigonia capros*, oceanic relative of our own boar-fish, conforms closely to the uliar deformation represented in Fig. 524.

Fig. 523. *Scorpaena* sp.

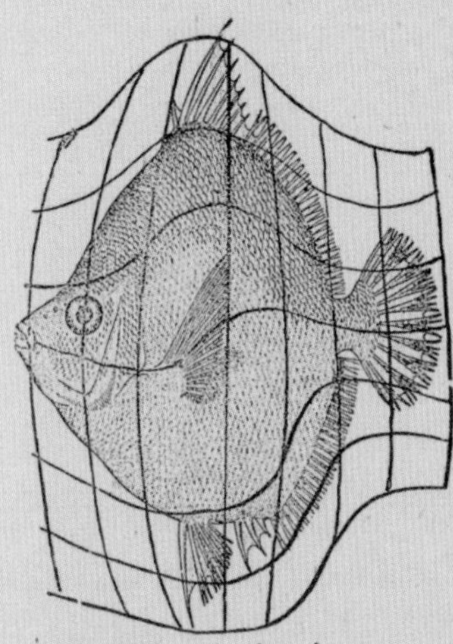

Fig. 524. *Antigonia capros.*

Fig. 525 is a common, typical *Diodon* or porcupine-fish, and in g. 526 I have deformed its vertical coordinates into a system of ncentric circles, and its horizontal coordinates into a system of rves which, approximately and provisionally, are made to resemble

30 Defying Social Convention

Maria Sibylla Merian, *Metamorphosis Insectorum Surinamensium*, 1705

Amsterdam: published at the expense of the author, 1705
Large folio, 507 × 370mm
Provenance: accessioned 1951
rff QL474.M2

Metamorphosis Insectorum Surinamensium is a remarkable book that pioneered entomological illustration and set the standard for future work. It was the first time insects had been depicted with their food plants and drawn to scale from living material. The artist, Maria Sibylla Merian (1647–1717), was a remarkable woman, earning a living from her painting in an age when this was generally a male profession, and she was also the first woman to visit a tropical country for the sole purpose of studying and illustrating the life of insects. She was hailed as the greatest nature artist of her day.

Maria had shown early interest in both art and entomology, and her father, Matthäus Merian the Elder (1593–1650), predicted that his daughter would make her name in art. Later, her stepfather, Jacob Marrell (1614–81), a Flemish flower painter and teacher, encouraged and taught the young girl to draw and paint. Defying social convention, she produced paintings of flowers, often including butterflies and other insects, as embroidery designs. She later trained her two daughters to draw and paint and published three illustrated volumes of flowers between 1675 and 1680. A further two-part work on butterflies followed, each part including 50 engravings of insects with their plants.

In 1685, after almost 20 years of marriage, she left her husband and joined a Protestant religious order in Friesland. Living with her daughters and mother in a castle owned by the governor of Suriname, she became interested in the natural history of South America. Later she moved to Amsterdam and in 1699, at the age of 52, Merian, with one of her daughters, set off on the journey to the colony of Dutch Guiana, now the Republic of Suriname. They spent two years in and around Paramaribo, making forays into the jungle to study, paint and collect tropical flora and fauna, before malaria and the hot, humid climate drove them back to Amsterdam to start the compilation of the volume. Two editions of *Metamorphosis Insectorum Surinamensium* were published in Amsterdam in 1705, in Dutch and Latin. It is the Latin edition, translated and with a descriptive footnote by Commelin, the director of the Amsterdam Botanical Garden, that the library holds. It contains 60 beautifully crafted plates with comments and descriptions. Many of the plants and insects illustrated were new to science.

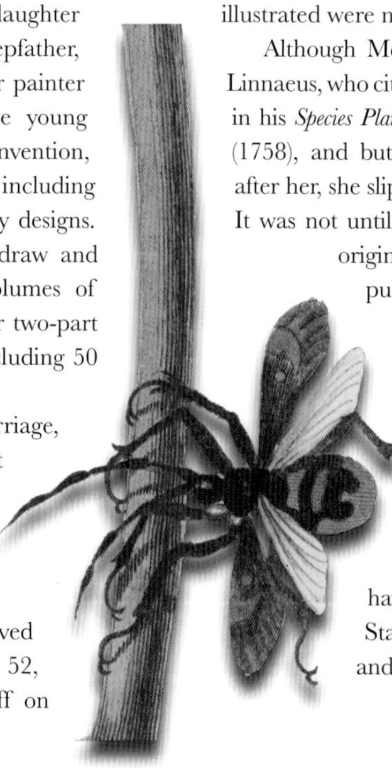

Although Merian's work was well known to Linnaeus, who cited many of her plants and insects in his *Species Plantarum* (1753) and *Systema Naturae* (1758), and butterflies and plants were named after her, she slipped into obscurity in later years. It was not until 1976, when her *Study Book* and original paintings on vellum were published by the St Petersburg Academy of Sciences, that a reappraisal of her work began. They had been purchased for Tsar Peter the Great by his Scottish physician Robert Eraskin a week before she died. In recent years exhibitions of her work have toured Britain and the United States. Merian's place in science and art has been restored.

Robert Mitchell

J. Mulder Sculp.

31 A Third Dimension

John Adamson, stereographic self-portrait, *c.*1845

Albumen print from a calotype negative, 87 × 160mm

Provenance: from Album 8, presented by the photographer to the Playfair family, 1860s; gift of Sir Edward Playfair, *c.*1970

ALB-8-88

Stereoscopic photography recreates the illusion of depth, the twin images seen by both eyes together interpreted by the brain to give an apparent third dimension of depth. A stereoscopic camera produces a pair of slightly dissimilar images, usually mimicking the distance between the human eyes, either by having twin lenses placed about the same distance apart and taking a pair of simultaneous exposures, or a single-lens camera being moved along a carefully measured curve a similar distance and taking two consecutive images. In turn, these twin images are placed side by side and are re-interpreted by the brain as three dimensional when viewed through a stereoscopic viewer.

In fact, stereoscopy (or binocular vision) was investigated during the 1830s, before the discovery of photography, by Charles Wheatstone (1802–75). He developed a viewing instrument using mirrors or prisms, now known as the reflecting stereoscope, which used outlined drawings. After the birth of photography in 1839, it was realized that photographic processes, such as the daguerreotype and calotype, could be given this 'third dimension'. Wheatstone apparently commissioned calotype photographs for his device from a number of photographic pioneers.

David Brewster (1781–1868) was approaching 60 years of age when he took up his first university position as principal of the United College in the University of St Andrews in 1838. By then regarded as a scientist of European standing, his early life had been spent supporting his growing family and his scientific investigations through scientific journalism. He had known the inventor of positive/negative photography since 1836, as he and W.H.F. Talbot (1800–77) shared a profound interest in optical science. Brewster came to St Andrews determined to transform the slumbering ancient university into a modern centre for promoting scientific endeavour. One of the methods for building up local support was through his formation of the St Andrews Literary and Philosophical Society, which, among its wide-ranging activities, provided a forum for the introduction of photography to Scotland. The Society's meetings became a venue where both calotypes and rival daguerreotypes were exhibited, and various members tried out these new and exciting 'black arts' with greater or lesser desgrees of success.

In this context, after photography had become established, David Brewster developed a second form of stereoscopic viewing device known as the 'lenticular stereoscope'. Recent attempts to reconstruct how this may have been developed have been heavily overwritten by David Brewster's annoyance at Wheatstone's undoubted priority and by his own increasingly acrimonious attempts to distinguish between the two forms of stereoscope. Nonetheless, Brewster himself identified this featured pair of photographs, first in an anonymous essay on photography in the *North British Review* for 1851, and then in his *Treatise on the Stereoscope*, which was published the following year and in which he writes: 'Dr Adamson of St Andrews, at my request, executed two binocular portraits of himself, which were generally circulated and greatly admired.'

Following Brewster's pioneering work, the stereo photograph used in conjunction with the stereoscope became a widely adopted form of parlour amusement in the 19th century, and its popularity led to the mass commercialization and dissemination of imagery in this unique photographic format throughout the modern world.

A.D. Morrison-Low

32 Sailing the Scottish Seas

Nicolas de Nicolay, *La navigation du Roy d'Escosse Iaques Cinquiesme du nom, autour du son Royaume, & Isles Hebrides & Orchades, soubz la conduicte d'Alexandre Lyndsay excellent pilote Escossois*, 1583

Paris: Gilles Beys, 1583
4to, 232 × 165mm
Provenance: purchased 1943
Typ FP.B83BN2

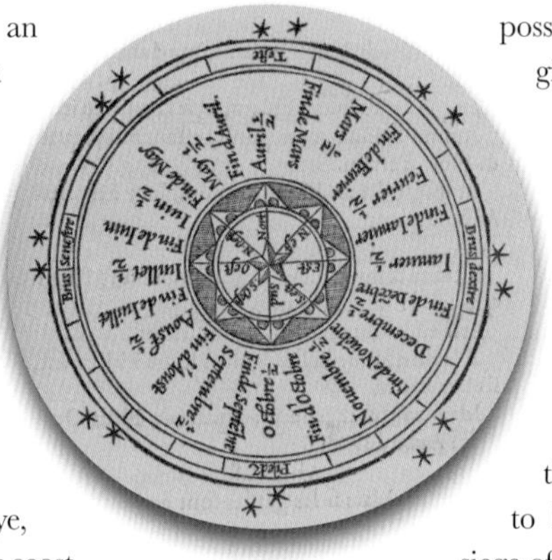

La Navigation du Roy d'Escosse is an updated translation into French of Alexander Lindsay's *A Rutter of the Scottish Seas* (1540). Both the *Rutter* and *La Navigation* describe in detail the Scottish coast, starting in the north of England at the Humber, continuing up the east coast past Leith, St Andrews, Aberdeen, the Orkney Islands and down the west coast past Skye, all the way down to the Galloway coast and on to the Isle of Man.

While Lindsay's work is thought to have been written to coincide with James V's naval expedition to 'daunt the Isles' in 1540, the significance of both the *Rutter* and *La Navigation* are wider than the king's attempt to flex his diplomatic muscle. The navigation of Scottish waters was of importance to numerous international parties as well as to the Scots. Weather conditions or political considerations frequently forced continental merchants to take the 'north about' route to and from their native countries (and thus avoid any hostile fleets waiting for them in the North Sea or English Channel). Such events occurred throughout the early 1540s when Scotland and France were engaged in a war against England. Thus navigational aids for the French were important not only to conduct trade but also to aid Scotland in the maritime war against her southern neighbour.

Remarkably, it was during a treaty negotiation in 1546 between Henry VIII of England and Francis I of France that Lindsay's *Rutter* fell into the possession of a Frenchman, Nicolay D'Arfeuille. After the negotiations Nicolay travelled to England where he stayed with the English Lord High Admiral, Sir John Dudley, who possessed a copy of the *Rutter*. Whether by gift or by deception, Nicolay returned to France with a copy, which was then translated from Scots into French for him by one John Fraser. A copy of the translation was passed on to the new king of France, Henry II, who gave it to Leon Strozzi, captain general of the French navy. This early French version (now lost) was put to use by the French squadron sent to St Andrews to help the Scottish authorities raise the siege of the bishop's castle there in 1547. Some 36 years later Nicolay presented a copy of a second French translation of the *Rutter* to Anne, duke of Joyeuse, admiral of the French fleet. Nicolay attributed the work to himself, although he acknowledged Alexander Lindsay within the title. Any contemporary reader would have seen this as acknowledgement enough, even if some more recent scholars might cry 'plagiarism'.

This volume is important in that it reflects the significance of an earlier work in Scots, albeit through translation into the more accessible lingua franca. Scholars of the *Rutter* have argued that later Dutch navigators such as Lucas Janszoon Waghener may have been influenced by the French version on the basis of similarities in descriptions of the Scottish coast between *La Navigation* and his *De Spieghel der Zeevaerdt* (1584).

The folding map, or chart, of Scotland included in *La Navigation* is of particular interest for its remarkable accuracy and the detail of the coasts and ports. It was not only the best outline of Scotland produced up to 1583 but was unsurpassed by any map in the 17th century and was still a valuable source for 18th-century cartographers.

Steve Murdoch

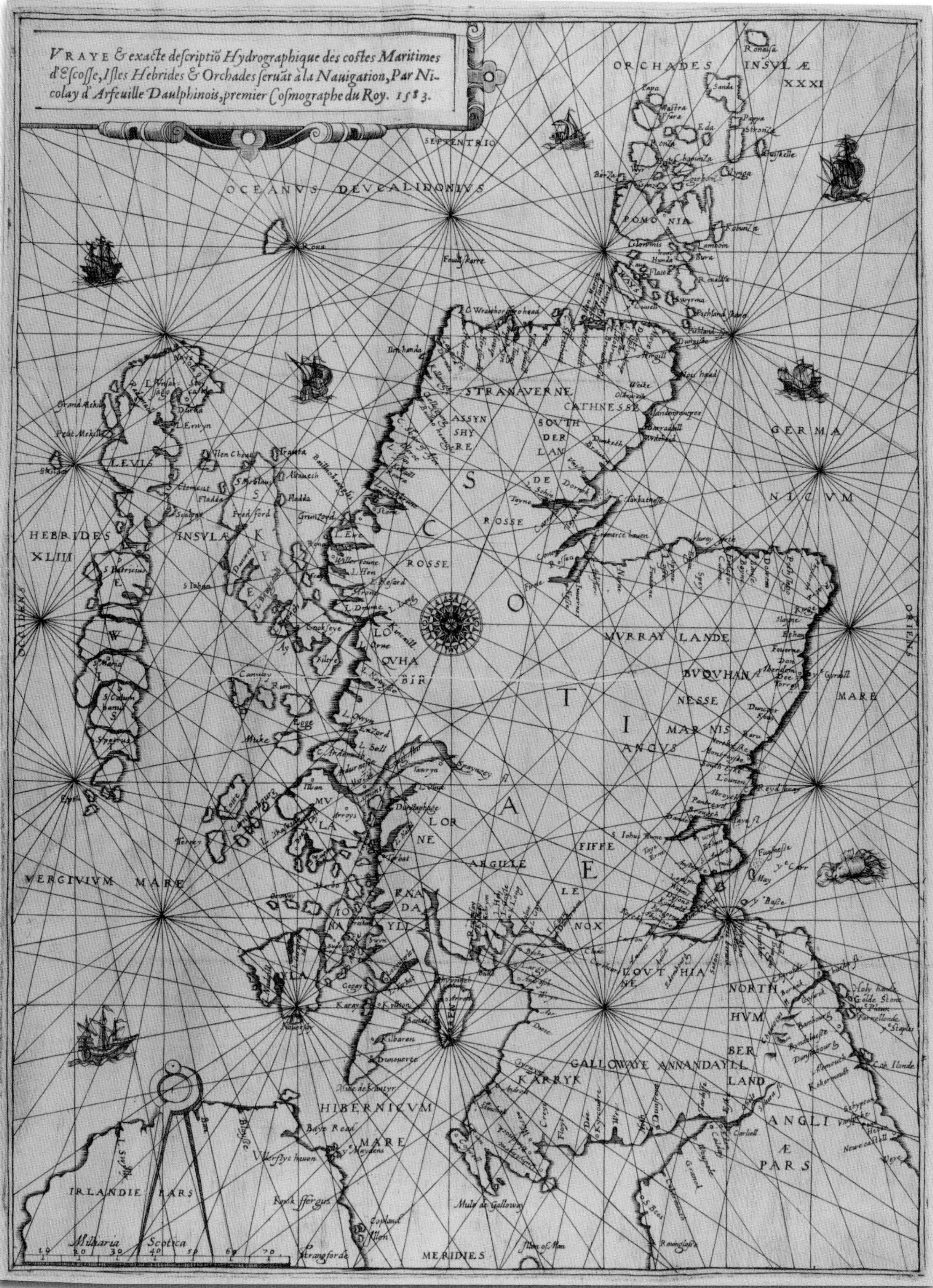
VRAYE & exacte descriptiō Hydrographique des costes Maritimes d'Escosse, Isles Hebrides & Orchades seruāt à la Nauigation, Par Nicolay d'Arfeuille Daulphinois, premier Cosmographe du Roy. 1583.
ORCHADES INSULÆ XXXI
SEPTENTRIO
OCEANUS DEUCALIDONIUS
POMONIA
STRANAVERNE
CATHNESSE
ASSYNSHYRE
SOUTHDERLANDE
GERMANICUM MARE
HEBRIDES XLIII
INSULÆ
LEVIS
SKYE
ROSSE
SCOTIAE
MURRAY LANDE
BUQUHAN NESSE
MARNIS
ANGUS
LORNE
FIFFE
ARGILLE
LENOX
LOUTHIANE
OCCIDENS
ORIENS
VERGIVIUM MARE
NORTHUMBERLAND
GALLOWAYE
ANNANDAYLL
KARRYK
HIBERNICUM MARE
IRLANDIE PARS
ANGLIÆ PARS
Militaria Scotica
10 20 30 40 50 60 70
MERIDIES

33 A Behemoth of Photographic Publishing

Five photographs by James Valentine & Sons: 'Forth Bridge Main Pier', 1888; 'Lednoch Dam, Comrie', registered 1958; 'Royal Exchange', Glasgow, registered 1878; 'Iona Cathedral and St Oran's Chapel', registered 1878; 'Royal Arch, Dundee', registered 1878

Various formats and sizes

Provenance: from the Valentine Collection, gifted by Valentine & Co., 1971

JV-10030; JV-D3440; JV-1600; JV-779[A]; JV-1626

In the middle of the 20th century if you purchased a picture postcard, it is likely that its publisher would have been Valentine & Sons of Dundee. The scene would most usually have been Scottish, though it could equally have been from anywhere in the British Isles and indeed from throughout the world. The photographic picture might be topographical, historical, an imposing country mansion, a scenic panorama, an episode from rustic life or even a titanic emblem of burgeoning industry. The postcard would serve as memento and souvenir, and you would be a consumer of that novel commodity, leisure and tourism.

James Valentine had been quick to see the potential of these parallel new industries of the Victorian period, photography and tourism. Born in 1815, he first established himself in the family business in Dundee as a printer, servicing the entrepreneurs of Scotland's fourth largest city with stationery. In 1851, barely a decade after the invention of photography in its modern form, he added portrait photography to his printing business, and the prosperous middle-class denizens of the city could find themselves immortalized in pictorial form. In the spirit of the age, this business prospered to the extent that Valentine could industrialize and commercialize the process. By 1855 he had created a magnificent glazed and light-filled factory for the processing of photographic prints. And, by 1870, he would become one of Britain's foremost producers of photographic panoramas and scenic views.

The company prospered in the hands of his sons. Whereas James Valentine had learned the mysteries of the daguerreotype in Paris during the late 1840s, his son, William Dobson Valentine, studied chemistry before coming under the tutelage of the English landscape photographer Francis Frith. These lessons would reap rewards as the company expanded into topographic views that would become the stock imagery of their viewcards, tourist memento packages and bespoke photographic albums. Following the death of James Valentine in 1879, William, together with his brother George Dobson Valentine, would develop the business into a titan of Victorian commerce. The company increasingly employed professional photographers to record the most emblematic views, and this output was reproduced using the most advanced of mechanical printing processes. As the Victorian period metamorphosed into 20th-century modernity, so Valentine & Sons became a behemoth of photographic publishing. The company expanded into greetings cards and books before its takeover and eventual closure in 1994.

The archive of over 120,000 photographic images held by the library, although only a fraction of Valentine's total production, is testament to the extraordinary achievements of the company throughout its near 150-year existence. From glass-plate negatives to photographic prints, albums and postcards, the collection presents a comprehensive record of this extraordinary enterprise. Among the finest of these photographic images, and including some canonical works of 19th-century photography, are to be found supreme examples of topographic, landscape, historical and genre scenes: photographic treasures that document and eulogize the natural and manmade world in a period of exceptional expansive optimism.

Tom Normand

FORTH BRIDGE, QUEENSFERRY MAIN PIER, AUG 15 1888. 10030 J.V.
ROYAL EXCHANGE, GLASGOW. 1351 J.V.
ROYAL ARCH. DUNDEE. 1626. J.V.

34 A Mediaeval Bestseller

Johannes de Sacro Bosco, *Sphaera Mundi*, 1490

Venice: [Bonetus Locatellus] for Octavianus Scotus, 1490
4to, 211 × 155mm
Provenance: presentation inscription to S.C. Cockerell, 1896; purchased 1953
Typ IV.A90LS

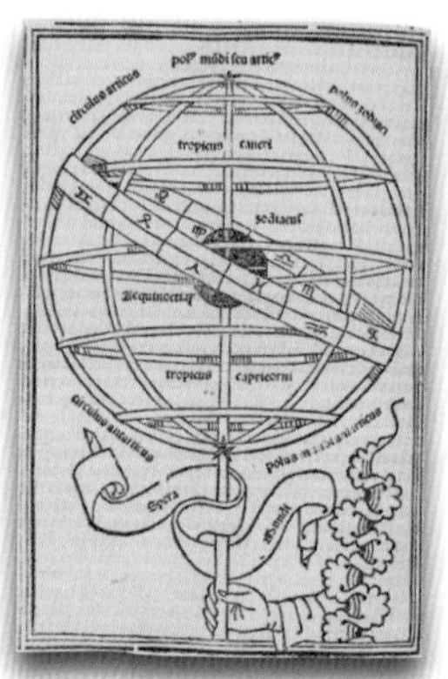

Venice was the greatest trading city of mediaeval Europe. Strategically placed between the city states of Italy and the urban economies of northern Europe, it was a natural conduit for the spices and luxuries of the Orient, a trade in which the city played a dominant role. In the 15th century its merchant entrepreneurs embraced the new world of print. The surplus capital of successful trading ventures was poured into the new art of printing, and within 30 years of Gutenberg's invention Venice had easily outstripped centres of the manuscript trade, such as Florence and Bruges, and the earliest centres of typography in Germany. Some 250 printers were active in Venice before 1501, including some of the greatest names of early printing.

Publishers in Venice made available to the reading public every type of book known to owners of mediaeval manuscripts. Among them were classics of scientific writing, including Sacro Bosco's *De sphaera*. Little is known of the author, Johannes de Sacro Bosco, but he is normally assumed to be English and to have taught in the University of Paris in the first decades of the 13th century. This work was his most important text. It treats of the earth and its relationship to other celestial bodies. From the movement of the stars Sacro Bosco derives proof that the earth was a sphere. The existence and popularity of this treatise is an important demonstration that this knowledge was widely disseminated in mediaeval Europe.

In the two centuries after its composition Sacro Bosco's treatise circulated widely in manuscript, and in the 15th century it rapidly made the transition to print. It was first printed, in Venice and Ferrara, in 1472, within three years of the introduction of printing to the Venetian republic. The copy owned by St Andrews is one of 34 editions published before 1501. Most were produced in the largest centres of European typography, north and south of the Alps, and this is no accident because the printing of such a text set particular challenges. In many respects the amalgamation of text and explanatory diagrams necessary in such scientific treatises was a great deal easier in the free-flowing context of a handwritten manuscript. The organization of the material on the page was far more difficult when text and woodcut diagrams had to be blended together. As we see here, Bonetus Locatellus, though an experienced and successful printer, had not yet fully mastered this art. An undifferentiated mass of Roman type contends uneasily with explanatory woodcuts of uneven quality.

The technical problems of production did not diminish the book's popularity, either with printers or the reading public. This was a mediaeval bestseller, and it continued to be republished in multiple editions through to the end of the 16th century. It was constantly re-edited and translated into several vernacular languages. The publication of Copernicus's milestone discoveries in 1543 brought no end to the demand for the great mediaeval scientific writings, and this enduring success of an earlier tradition of scientific knowledge, whether the mediaeval doctors or the classical authors of Greece and Rome, should give us pause for thought. Too often the invention of printing is associated with a progress-orientated view of the triumph of a new science based on empirical observation and the circulation of printed texts. But print could just as easily perpetuate outdated nostrums and entrench received wisdom, which, in the field of science and medicine, was often wholly wrong.

Andrew Pettegree

Quod aũt cælũ uoluaẽ ab oriẽte ĩ occidẽtẽ signũ ẽ. Stellæ q̃ oriunẽ ĩ oriẽte: semp eleuanẽ paulatĩ & successiue quousq; ĩ mediũ cæli ueniãt: & sũt sp ĩ eadẽ ꝓpinq tate & remotõe adiuicẽ: & ita sp se habẽtes tẽdũt ĩ occasũ cõtinue & uniformiter. Est & aliud signũ. Stellæ q̃ sẽ iuxta polũ arcticũ: q̃ nobis nũq̃ occidũt: mouẽẽ cõtiue & uniformiter circa polũ ɗscribẽdo circulos suos: & sp sẽ ĩæq̃li distãtia adiuicẽ & ꝓpĩqtate. Vnde p istos duos motus cõtiuos stellaꝝ tã tẽdẽtiũ ad occasũ q̃ nõ: patet q firmamẽtũ mouẽẽ ab oriẽte ĩ occidẽtẽ. DE cæli rotũditate.

Quod ãt sit cælũ rotũdũ: triplex ẽ rõ: silitudo: cõmoditas: & necessitas. Silitudo. n. quoniã mũdus sẽsibilis fcũs ẽ ad silitudinẽ mũdi archetypi: ĩ quo nõ ẽ prĩcipiũ neq; finis. Vnde ad huius silitudinẽ mũdus sẽsibilis hẽt formã rotũdã: ĩ q̃ nõ ẽ assignare prĩcipiũ neq; finẽ. Cõmoditas: qa oĩum corpoꝝ hysopimetroꝝ sphæra maxima ẽ: oĩum ẽt formaꝝ rotũda ẽ capacissima: quoniã igiẽ maximũ & rotũdũ: iõ capacissimũ: unde cũ mũdus oĩa cõtineat: talis forma fuit illi utilis & cõmoda. Necessitas: quoniã si mũdus eẽt alterius formæ q̃ rotũdæ. s. trilateræ uel q̃drilateræ uel multilateræ seq̃renẽ duo ĩpossibilia. s. q aliqs locus eẽt uacuus: & corpus sine loco: quoꝝ utrũq; falsũ est: sicut patet ĩ angulis eleuatis & circũuolutis. Itẽ sicut dicit Alfraganus si cælũ eẽt planũ: aliq̃ ps cæli eẽt nobis ꝓpinqor alia: illa. s. q̃ eẽt supra caput nr̃m: igr̃ stella ibi existẽs eẽt nobis ꝓpinqor q̃ existẽs ĩ ortu uel occasu: sed quæ nobis ꝓpinqora sũt maiora uidenẽ. ergo sol uel alia stella existẽs ĩ medio cæli maior uideri deberet q̃ existẽs ĩ ortu uel occasu: cuius cõtrariũ uidemus cõtigere. Maior. n. apparet sol uel alia stella existens ĩ oriẽte uel occidẽte q̃ ĩ medio cæli: sed cũ rei ueritas ita nõ sit: huius apparẽtiæ cã ẽ: q ĩ tpe hyemali uel pluuiali qdã uapores ascẽdũt ĩter aspectũ nr̃m & solẽ uel aliã stællã & cũ illi uapores sint corpus diaphanũ disgregãt radios nr̃os uisuales: ita q nõ cõpræhẽdũt rẽ ĩ sua naturali & uera q̃titate: sicut patet de denario ꝓiecto ĩ fũdo aq̃ lympidæ q pp similẽ disgregationẽ radioꝝ appet maioris q̃ suæ ueræ q̃titatis. Quod terra sit rotũda.

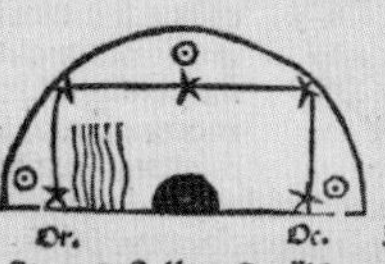

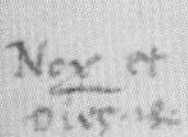

Quod etiã terra sit rotũda sic patet. Signa & stellæ nõ æq̃lr̃ oriunẽ & occidũt oĩbus hoĩbus ubiq; existẽtibus: sed prius oriunẽ & occidũt illis q sũt uersus occidentẽ uel uersus oriẽtẽ. & q citius & tardius oriunẽ & occidũt qbusdã: cã ẽ tumor terræ: quod bene patet p ea q̃ fiũt ĩ sublimi. Vna. n. & eadẽ eclypsis lunæ numero q̃ apparet nobis ĩ prima hora noctis: apparet orientalibus circa horã noctis tertiã. Vnde cõstat q prius fuit illis nox & sol prius eis occidit q̃ nobis. Cuius rei cã est tãtũ tumor terræ. q terra ẽt hẽat tũorositatẽ a septẽtriõe ĩ austꝝ: & ecõtra sic patet. Existẽtibꝫ uersus septẽtrionẽ q̃dã stellæ sẽ sẽpiternæ appitõis. s. q̃ ꝓpiq̃ accedũt ad polũ arcticũ. Aliæ uero sũt sẽpiternæ occultatõis sicut illæ q̃ sẽ ꝓpinq̃ polo ãtarctico. si igr̃ aliqs ꝓcederet a septẽtrione uersus austꝝ: ĩtãtũ posset ꝓcedere: q stellæ q̃ prius erãt ei sẽpiternæ appitõis: ei iã tẽderẽt ĩ occasum: & q̃to magis accederet ad austꝝ: tanto plus mouerẽẽ ĩ occasũ. Ille iteꝝ idẽ hõ iã posset uidere stellas q̃ prius fuerant ei sẽpiternæ occultatõis. Et ecõuerso cõtigeret alicui ꝓcedẽti: ab austro uersus septẽtrionẽ. huius aũt rei cã ẽ tãtũ tũor terre. Itẽ si terra eẽt plana ab oriẽte ĩ occidẽtẽ: tã cito orirẽẽ stellæ occidẽtalibꝫ q̃ oriẽtalibꝫ: qd patet eẽ falsũ. Itẽ si terra eẽt plana a septẽtriõe ĩ austꝝ & ecõtra: stellæ quæ essent alicui sempiternæ apparitiõis: sp apperẽt ei quocũq; ꝓcederet: qđ falsũ ẽ. Sed q plana sit pre nimia eius q̃titate hoĩum uisui apparet.

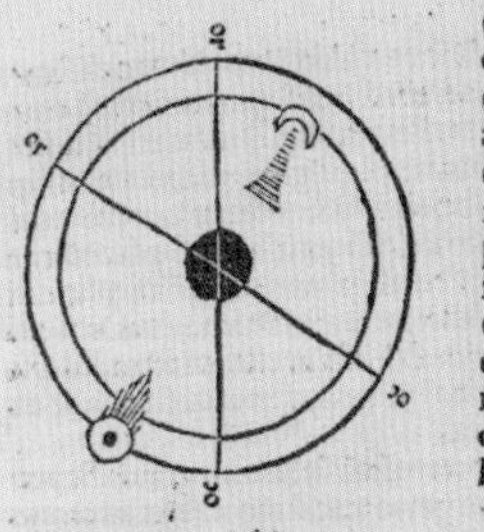

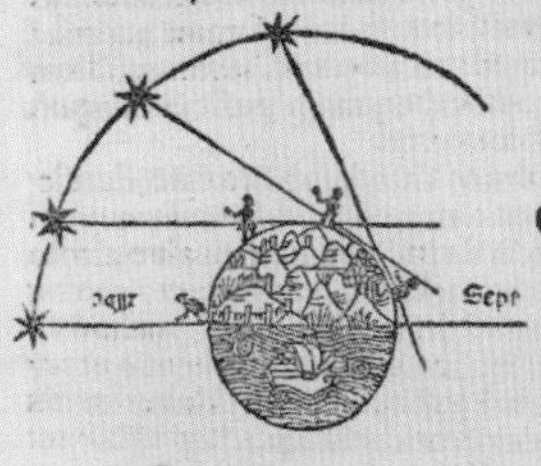

Quod aqua sit rotũda.

Quod ãt aq̃ hẽat tũorẽ & accedat ad rotũditatẽ sic patet. Põaẽ signũ ĩ littore maris & exeat nauis a portu: & ĩtãtũ elõgeẽ q oculus existẽs iuxta pedẽ mali nõ possit uidere signũ. Stãte uero naui oculus eiusdẽ existẽtis ĩ sũmitate mali: bene uidebit signũ illud. Sed oculus existẽtis iuxta pedẽ mali melius ɗbeẽt uidere signũ q̃ q ẽ ĩ sũmitate: sicut patet p lineas ab utroq; ad signũ: & nulla alia huius rei cã ẽ q̃ tũor aq̃. Excludaẽ. n. oĩa alia ĩpedimẽta: sicut nebulæ & uapores ascẽdẽtes. Itẽ cũ aq̃ sit corpꝫ hõgeneũ: totũ cũ p̃tibꝫ eiusdẽ erit rõis: sed ptes aq̃: sicut ĩ guttulis & roribꝫ herbaꝝ accidit: rotũdã naturalr̃ appetũt formã: ergo & totũ cuius sẽ ptes. Quod terra sit centꝝ mũdi.

Quod ãt terra sit ĩ medio firmamẽti sita sic patet. Existẽtibꝫ ĩ supficie terræ stellæ apparẽt eiusdẽ q̃titatis siue sint ĩ medio cæli: siue iuxta ortũ: siue iuxta occasũ: & hoc quia terra eq̃lr̃ distat ab eis. Si. n. terra magis accederet ad firmamẽtũ ĩ una pte q̃ in alia: aliqs existens ĩ illa pte supficiei terræ q̃ magis accederet ad firmamẽtũ nõ uideret cæli medietatẽ: sed hoc ẽ cõtra Ptolæmeũ & oẽs phõs dicentes q

35 Boundless Merry-making

Bull of Pope Benedict XIII, 1413

Parchment, 468 × 670mm, with lead bulla on bicoloured silk cords
Provenance: issued to the university
UYUY100

This is the document upon which the University of St Andrews asserts its legitimacy. The only survivor of six bulls (so called because of the lead *bulla* or seal used to authenticate such documents) issued at Peñiscola in Aragon on 28 August 1413, it affirms the charter of incorporation already issued by the bishop of St Andrews and authorizes the university to award degrees that licensed the graduates to teach in the disciplines of theology, canon and civil law, arts and medicine. The bulls arrived in St Andrews on 3 February 1414 and were greeted by magnificent celebrations. According to the contemporary chronicler Walter Bower, there were solemn services in the cathedral, grand processions of clergy and even street parties in which the citizens indulged 'in boundless merry-making and kept large bonfires burning in the streets … while drinking wine in celebration'. The first cohort of 11 students graduated only a few months later.

As early as May 1410 a small group of scholars had arrived in St Andrews to begin teaching. In February 1412 the bishop of St Andrews, Henry Wardlaw, provided a charter giving the fledgling institution the 'corporate' status of a university and establishing its administrative structure and formal relationship with the town. However, only papal or imperial authority could grant the essential right to award degrees and, with the authority of the king in parliament, an envoy was therefore dispatched to the papal court, probably in the latter months of 1412, resulting in the issuing of the crucial documents.

The entire process of foundation took place against a background of political turmoil. The Scots king, James I, had been captured by the English (with whom conflict was endemic in mediaeval times) shortly before his succession in 1406. He was not released until 1424, and his authority in the parliament that sent the embassy to the pope in 1412 was therefore wielded on his behalf by a regent (although the king had been personally consulted on the matter). Europe was also seriously divided by the great schism, which from 1378 to 1418 saw rival popes vying for authority over Christendom. By 1412 only Scotland and the Spanish kingdoms still supported the papacy of Pedro de Luna as Benedict XIII. France had withdrawn allegiance to him in 1407, and the welcome traditionally offered to Scottish students in France, particularly in Paris and Orléans, was waning. It was therefore important that Scotland had its own university. Moreover, it was in line with an increasing fragmentation of the European educational set-up, which in this period saw many 'national' universities established. St Andrews, the seat of the senior bishopric and where the great mediaeval priory was already a place of learning, was the obvious location. The scholars who started teaching in 1410 may indeed have been 'exiled' from Paris, but the foundation was not accidental: it was a calculated move in response to local and international events. Following the end of the schism the foundation of the university was upheld by the later popes, and this document, although coming from the hand of one whom history describes as an 'anti-pope', nonetheless remains our 'founding statute' and a priceless treasure of the university.

Norman H. Reid

Benedictus episcopus servus servorum dei : Ad perpetuam rei memoriam

[illegible]

Reverse of bulla, no. 35.

36 Falsified Philosophy

Lecture notes on dialectic by John Malcolm, *c.*1584–6

Paper, 145 × 93mm, in contemporary parchment binding
Provenance: purchased 1861
msBC59.M2

This small outline of the lectures on dialectic given by John Malcolm, a regent in St Leonard's College, is the earliest surviving evidence of what was actually taught at any Scottish university in the post-Reformation period. It is of particular value as evidence of the reaction towards the Protestant 'New Foundation' of the university, ratified by parliament in 1579, which adopted many of the features of the reform programme pioneered at the University of Glasgow between 1574 and 1577 by the Presbyterian educational and religious reformer Andrew Melville. A major component of Melville's educational programme was the adoption of the universal 'method' pioneered by the French educational reformer Peter Ramus (1515–72). This provided students with a simplified system of universal precepts to assist with learning any subject in the curriculum and was highly critical of Aristotle's traditional teachings on logic and philosophy. James Melville recorded in his diary that the regents in St Leonard's College, including Malcolm, reacted strongly against his uncle Andrew when the latter became principal of St Mary's College in 1580, protesting that 'thair bread-winner, thair honour, thair estimation, all was gean, giff Aristotle sould be sa owirharled in the heiring of thair schollars'. However, James claimed that his uncle persevered in his public lectures and easily won the regents over.

Malcolm's lecture notes show the tense reality behind Melville's optimistic appraisal of the situation. Provocatively entitled *Dianetica ad Aristotelis Scientiam non ad Rami Opinionem Continuatam* (Dialectic taught according to the wisdom of Aristotle, not the 'opinion' of Ramus), Malcolm's text offers a summary exposition of the central tenets of Aristotelian logic, oddly fused with references to Ramist terms and couched in a broadly Ramist framework. While Malcolm's notes show how far the tenets of Renaissance humanism had penetrated St Andrews by the end of the 16th century (being replete with extensive quotations from classical authors including Cicero, Ovid and Martial), their slightly confused nature suggests that Melville's arrival in St Andrews prompted a voguish appetite in the students for Ramism, to which Malcolm felt he had to pander. He seems to suggest this in his introduction, where he notes that even though he is teaching using the Ramist method, he believes it is 'a new school of falsified "philosophy"' and is 'unwilling to say that the dialectical opinion of Ramus' narrow system should be given priority, but that it should be reconciled with Aristotle's, [which is] broad, useful and necessary'.

Malcolm's notes lie within a context of a number of such items, from the mediaeval period onwards, which have been collected by the library over many years. This type of record always provides a fascinating insight into the academic life of the institution, and these particular notes say something important about how the new ideas associated with the 'Melvillian' reform plan were received in St Andrews. Malcolm critically appraises the value of the Ramist 'method' and finds it wanting in comparison with Aristotle, arguing that the focus of the former on practical application at the expense of in-depth philosophical training left students intellectually impoverished and unable to hold nuanced debate. His lecture notes clearly show that the process of adopting new intellectual modes at St Andrews in the post-Reformation period was one fraught with difficulty.

Steven John Reid

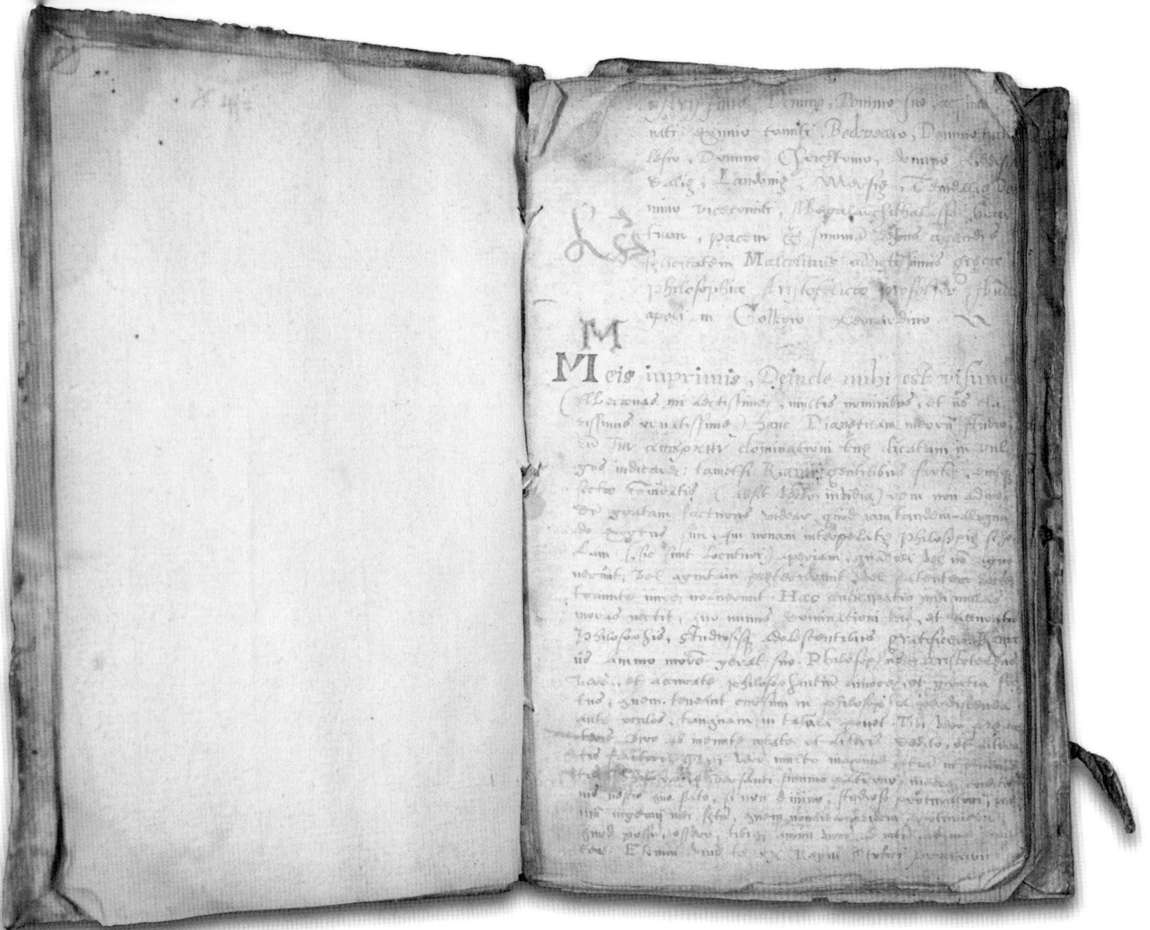

[illegible]

Andreapoli. Calend. Decemb. 1586

Consule quaeso boni forsan, maiora feremus

Nomine, Mecoenas, et mage digna tu[illegible]

Vive Deo, et patriae, Sceptrum unite R[illegible]

Laetos vive dies, nestoreosque, Vale.

Dominationi tuae addictissimus Malcolmus [illegible]

[illegible]NETICA ad Aristotelis [illegible]

entiam non ad Rami opinionem [illegible]

Auctore Malcolmo Scoto Graec. philo-

sophiae Aristotelicae professore Andreapoli

in Collegio Leonardino

PHILOSOPHIAE notatio est φιλία τῆς

σοφίας, id est amor sapientiae.

Definitio est γνῶσις θείων, καὶ ἀνθρωπίνων

πραγμάτων [illegible]

[illegible]

Andreapoli

37 Galileo and his Intellectual Property

Galileo Galilei, *Difesa*, 1607

Venice: Tomaso Baglioni, 1607
4to, 215 × 160mm
Provenance: from the library of James David Forbes, presented by George Forbes, 1929
For QB41.G2D5

The *Difesa* is a fascinating book. Not only does it show some of Galileo's thinking at the time about the structure of the universe, but it also gives great insight into Galileo's character and into the way in which science was conducted at the beginning of the 17th century.

Galileo wrote the *Difesa* as a strongly worded attack on Baldessar Capra, who had plagiarized his writings and was claiming to have invented a mathematical instrument that Galileo had invented many years earlier. Galileo, not one to miss a trick in belittling his opponent, uses considerable literary skill in attacking Capra, fully exploiting the fact that *capra* means 'goat' in Italian.

There are two parts to the text. In the first part Galileo responds to criticisms from Capra contained in *Consideratione astronomica circa la stella nona dell'anno 1604*, which was published in 1605. It concerned the appearance of a nova, which became visible on 9 October and continued to brighten. Galileo first observed the new star on 28 October, just a few days before it reached its maximum brightness on 1 November. Galileo, at this time a professor at Padua, delivered three lectures on the nova that were so popular that no hall in Padua was large enough to accommodate the audience that came. Capra claimed that he and his teacher, Simon Mayr, had been first to observe the nova (which was probably true) and made fun of Galileo for being so slow to spot it. He also reprimanded Galileo for not acknowledging their prior discovery in the lectures he had given on the nova in Padua. Galileo responded forcibly in the *Difesa*.

The second part of the *Difesa* contains Galileo's arguments to support his priority in inventing a geometrical and military compass and argues that Capra published a Latin version of Galileo's *Le operazioni del compasso geometrico e militare di Galileo* (1606) under his own name. In fact, Galileo had published *Le operazioni* as a witness to his prior claim for inventing the geometrical compass, so having the text stolen as well as the compass itself added insult to injury. Galileo rapidly took action against Capra. He requested depositions from well-known people who could vouch for his priority and used these as evidence before a panel set up by the University of Venice to judge his complaint against Capra. These depositions are reproduced in the *Difesa*. The panel supported Galileo and ordered all copies of Capra's book to be destroyed.

This copy was purchased in March 1845 from Canciani, a bookseller in Venice, by James David Forbes, later principal of the United College of the University of St Andrews. A note by Forbes is pasted inside the front cover, describing how he visited the public library in Venice to authenticate the handwritten inscription at the foot of the title page. It is indeed, as Forbes suspected, the hand of Galileo himself, presenting the book to Angelo Contarini, a Venetian noble. Only three of the dozen or so copies of the *Difesa* that are known to survive are inscribed in this way.

Edmund F. Robertson

DIFESA
DI GALILEO GALILEI
NOBILE FIORENTINO,

Lettore delle Matematiche nello Studio di Padoua.

Contro alle Calunnie & imposture

DI BALDESSAR CAPRA
MILANESE,

Usategli sì nella Considerazione Astronomica sopra la nuoua Stella del M DC IIII. come (& assai più) nel publicare nuouamente come sua inuenzione la fabrica, & gli usi del Compasso Geometrico, & Militare, sotto il titolo di

Usus & fabrica Circini cuiusdam proportionis, &c.

CVM PRIVILEGIO.

IN VENETIA, M DC VII.

Presso Tomaso Baglioni.

Al Clar.mo S. Angelo Contarini l'autore

38 Rivers of Liquid Fire

William Hamilton, *Campi Phlegraei: observations of the volcanoes of the two Sicilies*, 1776 and *Supplement*, 1779

Naples: [s.n.], 1776, 1779
Large folio, 458 × 325mm

Provenance: Auchincruive bookplate; from the library of Sir Steven Runciman, bequeathed 2000

C*ampi Phlegraei* (the fields of flame) is the area around the Bay of Naples, named because of the fiery eruptions of Vesuvius and the smouldering, sulphurous crater at Solfatara. An area to avoid, most people might think. Not Sir William Hamilton (1730–1803), diplomat, connoisseur, archaeologist, art collector and British envoy at Naples from 1764. Now remembered as the husband of Nelson's mistress, Emma Hamilton, he was hilariously depicted by the cartoonist James Gillray as a short-sighted connoisseur perusing artefacts that alluded to his wife's affair. Consenting cuckold he may have been, yet Hamilton was also a pioneer of modern vulcanology and the author of this magnificently illustrated folio volume, with text in English and French.

On his arrival at Naples in 1764 Hamilton established two residences, one at Naples and another on the slopes of Vesuvius between Pompeii and Herculaneum. At 7pm on Friday, 28 March Vesuvius began a particularly active period of eruptions, with flames, smoke, rocks, lava and ash spouting from the summit and threatening to destroy the settlements that had grown up since antiquity. Living so near to the action, Hamilton had many opportunities to observe the eruptions – often at alarmingly close quarters (one acquaintance who accompanied him on a foray across the fiery fields was badly burned). His observations were noted down and formed the basis for a series of letters to the president of the Royal Society in London, of which Hamilton was elected a Fellow in 1766. All five letters, comprising observations in the years 1764 to 1770, were then gathered and published in *Campi Phlegraei*, where they appeared with 54 hand-coloured illustrations by the British artist Peter Fabris. Fabris had accompanied Hamilton on his dangerous ventures to the summit of Vesuvius and sometimes down into the crater itself, sketching and taking notes of the scene of 'pale, bright fire'. His reward was to see his beautiful images of the Bay of Naples, Vesuvius and all kinds of eruptive activity reproduced in this extremely expensive and now rare volume.

Hamilton was what we would now call a geological 'revisionist'. Pompeii had persuaded the scientific establishment that volcanoes were uniquely destructive, but Hamilton sought to understand such 'dire misfortunes' in relation to what he called 'the great scale of nature'. As archaeologists uncovered the remains of Pompeii's streets, houses and citizens with fractured skulls, Hamilton concluded that they were the unlucky victims of 'operations … intended perhaps for … the benefit of future generations'. Looking around, Hamilton concluded (rightly) that volcanic ash made the landscape wonderfully fertile and that volcanoes and subterranean fire were vital to the geological life of the planet.

And Hamilton could write. While the illustrations capture the awesome power of the volcano, his prose has the sparky energy of 'a girandole of red-hot stones', while the quivering of the ground is likened to 'the timbers of a water-mill'. The earth moved for Sir William Hamilton, too.

Nicholas Roe

39 Sunshine: The Very Currency of Photography

Letter from William Fox Talbot to James David Forbes, 1839

Paper, folded to 316 × 199mm
Provenance: deposited by Forbes family, 1968
msdep7/Incoming Letters/1839

A remote and declining backwater in 1839, St Andrews extraordinarily emerged as one of the most powerful forces in introducing the new art of photography. Sir David Brewster, the freshly appointed principal of the United College of St Salvator and St Leonard, was close friends with William Henry Fox Talbot, the Wiltshire scientist who invented photography in 1834. Talbot, diverted by more pressing scientific and literary activities, was shocked in January 1839 by news from Paris that Louis Jacques Mandé Daguerre had a similar invention. With no way of knowing that Daguerre's approach using silver plates would be short-lived, while his images on paper presaged the future of photography, Talbot hastily exhibited his 1834–5 examples at London's Royal Institution on 25 January. Within the week his first paper on photography was read before the Royal Society.

One of the many interesting holograph letters held in the St Andrews collections outlines the situation Talbot faced. Written on 27 February 1839 to James David Forbes, Professor of Natural Philosophy in Edinburgh, it is the earliest known surviving letter between the two men:

> *I beg your acceptance of the inclosed photograph representing a gauze ribband –; I believe it is fixed … if the sunshine should injure it I will change it for another … There are however various minutiae, which if attended to improve the results. The only objection I can possibly have to Sir D. Brewster's showing the few specimens I sent him, is, that they give no adequate idea of the method, or of any part of it, being in fact the only things that I happened to have disposable the morning I sent them.*

Talbot was then in London, attending scientific meetings and distributing examples of early photographs whenever possible, soon exhausting his supply of pre-1839 images. Of all the factors stacked against Talbot in these early days, the weather was one of most vexatious. The very currency of photography was sunlight, and the depths of a British winter were never encouraging for this, with 1839 being unusually gloomy.

Forbes endorsed the letter 'Mr Fox Talbot / Feb. 1839 / With Photogenic Drawing', but sadly the 'inclosed photograph representing a gauze ribband' is no longer with the letter. On 26 February Talbot had made '3 ribbons, 5 stripes'. He 'fixed' only half of these, using a chemical solution to stabilize the image against the action of light. Seven were sent out to colleagues, including his fellow photographic experimenter, Sir John Herschel, the botanist John Lindley and the one to Forbes. Talbot kept the last one for himself, and, amazingly, the image survives today in the Smithsonian Institution's National Museum of American History in Washington, D.C. It must be virtually identical to the one sent to Forbes.

Talbot alerted Forbes to his published descriptions, but his caution that 'various minutiae … if attended to improve the results' was prescient. Brewster and his colleagues in St Andrews laboriously explored and mastered these minutiae, becoming the most accomplished early photographers in the world. Collaboratively, Talbot and his St Andrews colleagues made their 'fresh experiments' and rapidly improved his process on the familiar and versatile medium of paper, leading to the negatives and multiple prints that were to define photography right down to the current digital age.

Talbot and Forbes became lifelong correspondents, and 17 letters between them are known to have survived, ten of them at St Andrews (see http://foxtalbot.dmu.ac.uk). In the period of 1855–7, while Talbot was resident in Edinburgh, they exchanged scientific instruments and information, including Talbot's new invention of photographic engraving, which eventually would successfully merge photography with the printing press.

Larry J. Schaaf

44 Queen Anne St. London
Feb. 27. 1839

Dear Sir

Your letter was only forwarded to me today, or I should have replied to it sooner — I beg your acceptance of the inclosed photograph representing a gauze ribband —: I believe it is fixed, but you can try whether it is or not; if the sunshine should injure it I will change it for another. I described my process in its most essential particulars to the Royal Society last Thursday; and the account was copied into the Literary Gazette & Athenaeum of Saturday — There are however various minutiae which if attended to improve the results. The only objection I can possibly have to Sir D. Brewster's showing the few specimens I sent him, is, that they give no adequate idea of the method, or of any part of it, being in fact the only things that I happened to have

40 Making the Circles

Letter from John Row to his uncle, 1691

Paper, folded to 292 × 176mm
Provenance: accessioned mid-20th century
msLF1117.R6

John Row was a student in St Leonard's College in the University of St Andrews from 1678, graduating with an MA in 1682 and returning as a regent in January 1691. This letter was written to his uncle in August of that year, in response to a request for 'ane account of the Order & Disciplin of this Colledge'.

Classes were very small – when Row matriculated there were only 11 in his class – and students were young, often aged only 14 or 15, although college statutes decreed that they had to be at least 16 and 20 respectively to receive a bachelor's and a master's degree. A student had to apply to a regent for entry to his class, where he would remain for his entire period of study. The routine was rigorous, with students expected to be up at 5am, kept under supervision all day, with regular prayers, mealtimes and studies, and in bed by 9pm. Both masters and scholars lived in the college, and Row would have taken his turn as Hebdomadar, responsible for discipline of the students, a role that required him to 'perlustrat' around the college twice a day, checking that all the students were inside and gainfully occupied. All teaching and all conversation were meant to be conducted in Latin, and fines were imposed for speaking English.

Each master rebuked his own scholars over private questions of discipline, such as negligence in studies, but more serious lapses were punished by the principal and other masters. Row mentions such offences as swearing, absence from public prayers, cursing, playing at forbidden games, cards and dice (football was deemed unsuitable for students, while golf and archery were acceptable pastimes) or occasioning a brawl or tumult. Punishment was 'according to the demerit of the crime'. James Millar, a contemporary of Row, was expelled from the college for fighting, and his signature was cut out of the matriculation record.

Row gives a comprehensive picture of the process of examining for, and conferral of, the degree of Master of Arts. Examinations were by oral disputation, defending or opposing a question or thesis, rather than by written assessment. Each student might be examined for up to four hours, and, along with many orations by the regents, this public process could take up to four days. After a day of deliberation the chancellor and regents would 'make the circles', an old system of ranking the students according to merit. Conferral of the coveted Master's degree proceeded with great applause, which 'exceits the students all along their course, yea and the masters too, to a great dole of desirable Emulation'.

Fees and celebrations made graduation a costly process, and many students regarded it as an unnecessary expense. It was probably only important for those such as Row, who were embarking on an academic or ecclesiastical career. His admission as professor of philosophy on 15 January 1691 survives within the university muniments, as does an extensive set of notes of his philosophical dictates taken down by Patrick Bayne in 1694–5. He was a regent at Edinburgh University by 1695, a post he held until 1700. The Senate minutes of 1711 record Row's request for a diploma to prove he had studied and taught both Greek and philosophy at St Leonard's, presumably to allow him to further his career elsewhere. His vivid and detailed description of the early days of his career, however, offers a rare insight into the ordinary life of a student of the time.

Maia Sheridan

circles (for so many as are called-upon together, primus ultimus & ultimus primus do make-up a circle) which are made with respect to the accomplishments of the Candidati, viz: those who have Acquit themselves best in all the parts of the publick Examinadus & Disputs are, ordinarly, put-in the first, or highest circle, & some times there will be one or two, who do give proof of more than ordinar preg-nancie & Endumments, called wt great Applause to receive the Degree Ante om-nium circulum: This method of Conferring the Degree exceits the Students all-along their course, yea & the Masters too, to A great dale of desirable Emu-lation: for A regent who takes-up the Bajans keeps the same Scholers, & first teaches them Greek, & thereafter all the parts of philosophie (yet not-withstanding new Scolers may, & ordinarly do Enter with ym every year) till at last after four years they receive the Degree of Mrs of Arts, together with the Candi-dati or Magistrands of the old Colledge: And then these two regents take-up the Bajans again at the Downsitting of the Colledges. There are severall other publick Exercises in the Universitie both for Mastrs & Scoolers, which would be too long to be here fully Enumerated such as, the Commun Theam by the Semies to be made in Greek & by the Bajans in latin, prescribed to them by the Regents of Another Colledge; The Monethly Disputs in the New Colledge, in the publick Scools of the University, where all the Mastrs in the Universitie of whatever character or profession do per vices Sustain theses, & if the Sustainer have Scholers (for the principal masters, or heads of the colledges, have none) they do Sustain his theses, & he is preses: The publick lessons of the professor of Mathematicks in the sd Scools; The pub-lick lessons of Our professor of Humanitie in our Commun Scools etc: There is A great Solemnitie in the Universitie once in the year at the Election of the Rector. I forbear to give any account of the New Colledge, in which there is observed An Excellent Order & method, wt many publick Exercises for Students in Divinitie. There is little difference betwixt the order of the old Colledge & that of this, Excepting only that in the old Colledge, the Students have none of these weekly Orations, on the Saturnday mornings, which, I have Already said, Our Students have. As to the Disciplin of this Colledge In one word (because I have already exceeded the bounds of A letter) Each Mastr dos, according to his own Discretion, Rebuck or Correct his own Scholers, for all privat faults, such as Negligence in his Studies etc: Publick faults, such as Absence from publick prayers, Speaking of En-glish, Swearing, Cursing, playing at forbidden games, cartes dyce etc: Being the Occation of Broils or Tumults in the Colledge; Are punished in the publick Scools, by the principall & all the other Mastrs, According to the demerit of the Crim & customs of the Collage, By pecunniary Mulcts, wheep-ing, by one or more, & in extraordinary cases, by all the Masters, & for hyonous offences by Extrusion. I only add for Conclusion, that it will be proper for any Students from England to have A Direction from their friends to the Regent of that Class, to which its proper for him to Enter, And if they be not resolved there-anent, let him be directed to all the masters in general that they by mutual content may enter him or them to that class, to which it may be proper to Enter them wt respect to their proficiencie in their Studies before there comeing here. I can add no more here but that I am Reverend Sir Your Nephew & humble Servant

Ro: Ront.

41 War and Peace

George M. Cowie, 'Gas mask fitting, St Andrews', 1939

Negative, 35mm
Provenance: from the G.M. Cowie Collection, gift of the photographer, 1981
GMC-FE394

The negatives of St Andrews freelance press photographer George Cowie resonate as historical documents far beyond the town in which he lived. There remain 60,000 of his original negatives, which span a period of over half a century from the early 1930s to his death in 1982. Among the car smashes, plane crashes and railway accidents, right through to church sales of work, the everyday events of life are represented, cast into relief by pinnacles of world interest. An unannounced journey by Winston Churchill in 1940 to meet General Sikorski in St Andrews, visits by literary figures as diverse as J.M. Barrie and Mikhail Sholokhov and the opening of three of the great road bridges of Britain, Kincardine, Forth and Tay, all find their place in this archive.

The successful press photographer must have instantaneous recognition of the publishable news photograph, and George Cowie's shot of a small boy being fitted with a gas mask in St Andrews Town Hall on 5 March 1939 is testament both to his ability as a photojournalist and to the role he played in personalizing the story of this community. The wide-eyed boy immediately engages the viewer, and the repeating angles of the bodies of the fitters take the eye to the main centre of interest. Gas masks were issued in St Andrews over three days in each of three centres, a fact that demonstrates a general fear on the part of all the prospective combatants of the looming Second World War. The poignancy of sentiment embodied in this boy's expression, which would not have been lost on the viewers of Cowie's image, was doubtless heightened by the knowledge that all the main nations held large stockpiles of the various gases, despite the Geneva Convention of 1925 having banned their use.

The Cowie and Govan business was in fact started not by George Cowie, but by Beatrice Govan, who had so impressed her first employer that he made her a partner in his business in North Berwick, Day & Govan. When her childhood friend, George Cowie, became disillusioned with joinery and then gardening, she suggested he think of photography and no doubt also persuaded him to learn the ropes of press photography. George and Beatrice married in June 1930 and spent their honeymoon in St Andrews. A year later, perhaps especially tempted by the opportunities the town offered for selling golfing photographs to the press, they set up their own business in Market Street. Their work covered a wide range of photojournalism and studio photography, with golf-related subjects occupying about a quarter of their production. Beatrice mostly saw to the studio work, the processing, and looked after the retail shop, but occasionally they did outdoor jobs together and may be found in the backgrounds of each other's shots. They occupied their final premises at 131 South Street from 1935 until they were sold in 1981.

Representative of photojournalistic practice in the mid-20th century, the collection vividly illustrates rural and town life in Scotland. The images are both common in their everyday nature and yet exceptional because of their purposed representation of events for publication. Because of the importance of St Andrews as a centre of both recreation and higher learning, Cowie's photographs provide a matchless insight into the everyday life of a community, while at the same time being steeped in the context of international events and the people who would shape them.

Robert Smart

42 Extraordinary Taste and Skill

Four photographic portraits by John Adamson, 1860s

Albumen prints, various sizes

Provenance: Album 5: gift of Miss Lowson, 1947. Album 8: presented by the photographer to the Playfair family, 1860s; gift of Sir Edward Playfair, *c.*1970. Album 13: acquired from South Court, St Andrews, 1916

ALB5-43, ALB8-16, ALB8-30, ALB13-15 (clockwise from top left)

Described in 1867 as 'an amateur [photographer] of extraordinary taste and skill', John Adamson (1810–70) was one of the original 'disciples' in Scotland of Henry Fox Talbot (1800–70), the inventor of negative–positive paper photography. Born into a farming family near St Andrews, Adamson trained as a doctor before sailing to China as a ship's surgeon. On returning to Scotland in 1835, he established himself in St Andrews where he developed links with the university and with David Brewster, principal of the United College. Later in his life, Adamson specialized in public health, promoting sanitary reform in Fife.

Adamson and his younger brother Robert (1821–48) produced many of the earliest photographs taken in Scotland and, in November 1842, sent a presentation album containing specimens of their work to Talbot, 'in testimony of the great pleasure we have derived from your discovery'. Robert died in 1848, but John continued to practise photography during the 1850s and 1860s. Working with the wet collodion process, he collaborated with his pupil and assistant Thomas Rodger (1832–83) to produce an impressive body of photographic portraits.

The present portraits are representative of Adamson's mature work, thought to be from the early to mid-1860s – two of women, one young and somewhat uncertain, and the other poised, remote and fashionable, and two portraits of men, one mature, confrontational and somewhat ominous, and the other mild, venerable and distinguished. The older woman evidently moved in 'society'. Her elaborate dress, hat, shawl and veil function as a carapace, and the fact that she appears in profile further distances her from the viewer. The profile was a classical portrait type that permitted viewers to scrutinize sitters without contravening principles of decorum. The young woman's identity is not known, but the portrait suggests that she considered the sitting to be a special occasion, one that she approached somewhat coquettishly. By catching the viewer's gaze, she flouts convention – perhaps her photograph was to be a keepsake for her sweetheart. The men are linked in so far as both belong to the Playfair dynasty. The elderly gentleman is James Playfair (1791–1866), youngest son of the Rev. James Playfair (1738–1819), principal of the United College at St Andrews from 1799 until his death. A prominent merchant in Glasgow, he looks to higher things, while holding a copy of *The Scotsman*. The young man, whose folded arms present an impregnable barrier to the viewer, is Robert Lambert Playfair (1828–99). Born in St Andrews, he was the third son of Playfair's eldest brother and achieved the rank of lieutenant-colonel in the Indian army before becoming consul-general of Algeria in 1867.

As a group, these four photographs provide a synoptic view of society in Scotland in the early 1860s, portraying a diverse spectrum – male and female, young and old – and hinting at the range of accomplishment that emanated from this small corner of Scotland. John Adamson's photographic oeuvre provides a vivid and rarely encountered authenticity of personal expression on the part of the sitter. It suggests a familiarity between the photographer and his subject and communicates intelligently their individual personalities.

Such intimate images suggest collaboration, and its expression through this new medium was exceptional during photography's early days, underlining John Adamson's pivotal role as a pioneering force in the development of photographic practice in Scotland.

Graham Smith

43 Wild Places

Two photographs by Robert Moyes Adam: 'W. Finlayson, stalker and resident of Alltbeithe with postman, Glen Affric', 1930; 'Interior of black house (the dwelling of the weaver, Mr McInnes), Scarp, west Harris', 1937

Glass negatives, 118 × 163mm
Provenance: from the R.M. Adam Collection, gift of D.C. Thomson & Co., 1987
RMA-H2287; RMA-H5630

Adam was unquestionably the finest Scottish landscape photographer of his time. Working in black and white, he was without peer until the later 20th century, when Hamish Brown and Patricia Macdonald each began their work with modern cameras and using colour. His achievement in portrayal of wild places foreshadows by decades the work of Ansel Adams in America. He was also an expert photographer of the Gaels and their home, just as the distinctive character of the Hebridean world was about to vanish. Both art historian and social historian find his work compelling.

Adam was a son of the manse, born in 1885 in Lanarkshire, brought up and educated at Edinburgh, including a time at art college. His first job was in the Royal Botanic Gardens, helping to prepare illustrations for lectures, and he was soon appointed botanist at the gardens, a job he retained all his life. The camera was not his profession but his passion – late in life people found him grumpy but transformed when speaking of his art and wild places. He was concerned about destruction by development, and when in 1929 a hydroelectric scheme was planned in Glen Affric he sent every Scottish MP four of his prints to show them what beauty was threatened. The scheme was eventually built anyway, but undertaken with more care and consideration for the environment than any other in Scotland. Some of the credit for this must go to Adam.

The distinctive character of Adam's work is based on the equipment he used and his manner of working. From 1908 until he gave up photography due to ill health in 1956, he most frequently used the same half-plate camera with glass plates of 4¾ inches by 6½ inches (121 × 165mm), mounted on a wooden tripod, the whole weighing about 30 pounds (13.6kg). With this device he took most of his 15,000 negatives. He worked deliberately, often planning a trip for months in advance and composing a picture with every possible consideration to light, angle and content. Despite the weight of his camera, he often carried it long distances (he told a friend that not one picture in 50 was taken near a road) and chose a high elevation to make the most effective landscape shot. He characteristically used a small aperture and long exposure to get the maximum depth of field and sharpness of detail. Adam's concentration on the landscape tended to result in over-exposed skies, so he often photographed the sky separately and blended the two together in production. Sometimes he used a sky picture from a different place altogether. This technique also meant that none of Adam's pictures could be action shots, and his waterfalls were a flow of milky white.

Photographs taken, Adam, skilled in the artistry of the darkroom, then spent a great deal of time completing his magic. He worked slowly (the prints were as long as half an hour in the developing bath) to enhance the drama of the finished print. Even in 1968 it was noticed that 'skilful laboratory workers today can produce little worthwhile off his negatives if they try to print them by fast, up-to-date techniques', which remains true to this day.

Adam died in 1967. His negatives had been purchased in 1958 by D.C. Thomson of Dundee, which had published many of them in the *Scots Magazine* and other journals and which later generously donated them to the library, where they remain a precious and frequently used resource.

T.C. Smout

44 Hours of Reading and Meditation

Selected works of Augustine of Hippo, *c.*1190

Parchment, 402 × 290mm, in re-covered mediaeval oak boards

Provenance: ownership inscription of mediaeval priory of St Andrews; appears in St Leonard's College library catalogue, 18th century

msBR65.A9

Only one manuscript book from the St Andrews cathedral priory now remains in St Andrews, the other six known survivors being in the Helmstedt Collection of the Herzog August Bibliothek, Wolfenbüttel, and in the Bibliothèque Nationale de France, Paris. This is a massive late 12th-century miscellany of shorter theological works by St Augustine of Hippo (354–430), including his *Retractationes*, which may reasonably be supposed to have been compiled for the use of the Augustinian canons of St Andrews in their hours of reading and meditation. Written in the same caroline minuscule hand throughout its 325 leaves, it bears its text in careful and consistent double columns on each folio, with rubrics in red and blue and regular decoration of initial capitals at significant places within the text. Sadly, the most prestigious illuminated initials at the beginning of the most important works have all been excised by an unknown vandal from a previous generation. As is normal for books belonging to institutional libraries, it bears an ownership inscription – in this case a 13th-century hand proclaims that it was owned by the monastery of St Andrew the apostle in Scotland. Around the time of the Reformation it seems to have passed into lay hands, identifiable from their annotations on the work: James Wynram, Margaret Lauder his 'sweetheart' and her brother William Lauder, laird of Halltoun, from whose family it seems to have passed to St Leonard's College. It is likely to have been transferred to the custody of the library along with other college books in the late 18th century.

For today's teachers, students and researchers this manuscript offers an invaluable resource. For researchers it offers evidence of the transmission of these works of St Augustine, specifically as to how accurately their text has been copied, where and when they are known, and thus the routes of transmission and readership. For teachers and students it is a resource for the study of palaeography and codicology and has been so used within the university over at least the last 30 years. The opportunity to handle and engage with such an impressive original has been the highlight of manuscript studies for many cohorts of students. They have been able to examine holes in the parchment showing that the animals whose skin was used suffered from warble fly, stitchmarks, the preparation of the writing surface with ruling and pricking (showing what lines were intended to be ruled to guide scribes in writing text), the layout of the text on the page, the use of colour, guide letters and catchwords and the minutiae of letter formation, scribal correction and marginal annotation. All this within repaired original mediaeval oak boards covered in pigskin with strap and pin fastening as is seen in images of any monastic scriptorium.

The book as we have it is now incomplete, since the quire signatures tell us that four gatherings are missing before folio 50. The grouping of texts within sets of predominantly eight-leaf gatherings for binding may imply that it was originally intended to be bound in two volumes, with the second volume to begin at the present folio 180; a gap before the text beginning on folio 146 might suggest a miscalculation by the scribe, and further observations may yet tell us more. This magnificent manuscript, then, still protects some of its secrets, but its identifiable local provenance and the wealth of tangible evidence it provides for manuscript production and use offer a tantalizingly personal link with the man who wrote it in St Andrews over eight centuries ago and with those who have savoured its contents ever since.

Clive R. Sneddon

Incipit annotatio sci augustini epi plurimorum operum. Incipiunt capitula.

De achademicis libri .iii.
De beata uita. lib. i.
De ordine. libri .ii.
De soliloquiis. libri .ii.
De inmortalitate anime. lib. i.
De moribus sce ecclesie catholice et de moribus manicheorum lib. ii.
De anime quantitate. lib. i.
De libero arbitrio. libri .iii.
De genesi aduersus manicheos. libri .ii.
De musica. libri .vi.
De magistro. lib. i.
De uera religione. liber .i.
De utilitate credendi. lib. i.
De duabus animabus. liber .i.
Acta contra fortunatum manicheum. lib. i.
De simbolo uel fide. liber .i.
De genesi ad litteram. lib. i.
De sermone dni in monte. libri .ii.
Psalmus contra partem donati.
Contra epistolam donati heretici. liber .i.
Contra adimantum manichei discipulum. lib. i.
Expositio quarundam propositionum ex epistola ad romanos. lib. i.
Expositio epistole ad galathas. lib. i.
Epistole ad romanos inchoate expositio. lib. i.
De diuersis questionibus .lxxxiii. lib. i.
De mendacio. lib. i.
Ad simplicianum epm. libri .ii.
Contra epistolam manichei quam uocant fundamenti. lib. i.
De agone xpiano. lib. i.
De doctrina xpiana. libri .iiii.
Contra partem donati. libri .ii.
Confessionum. libri .xiii.
Contra faustum manicheum. lib. xxxiii.
Contra felicem manicheum. libri .ii.
De natura boni. lib. i.
Contra secundinum manicheum. lib. i.
Contra hylarium. lib. i.
Questiones euangelii. libri .ii.
Annotationes in iob. lib. i.
De cathezizandis rudibus. lib. i.
.xli. De trinitate. lib. xv.
.xlii. De consensu euangelistarum. libri .iiii.
.xliii. Contra epistolam parmeniani. libri .iii.
.xliiii. De baptismo. libri .vii.
.xlv. Contra quod attulit centurius a donatistis. lib. i.
.xlvi. Ad inquisitiones ianuarii. libri .ii.
.xlvii. De opere monachorum. lib. i.
.xlviii. De bono coniugali. lib. i.
.xlix. De sca uirginitate. lib. i.
.l. De genesi ad litteram. lib. xii.
.li. Contra litteras petiliani. lib. iii.
.lii. Ad cresconium grammaticum partis donati. lib. iiii.
.liii. Probationum et testimoniorum contra donatistas. lib. i.
.liiii. Contra nescio quem donatistam. lib. i.
.lv. Ammonitio donatistarum de maximianistis. lib. i.
.lvi. De diuinatione demonum. lib. i.
.lvii. Questiones exposite contra paganos. lib. i.
.lviii. Expositio epistole iacobi ad .xii. tribus. lib. i.
.lix. De peccatorum meritis et remissione et de baptismo paruulorum ad marcellinum. lib. iii.
.lx. De unico baptismo contra petilianum ad constantinum. lib. i.
.lxi. De maximianistis contra donatistas. lib. i.
.lxii. De gratia testamenti noui ad honoratum. lib. i.
.lxiii. De spiritu et littera ad marcellinum. lib. i.
.lxiiii. De fide et operibus. lib. i.
.lxv. Breuiculus collationis cum donatistis. lib. i.
.lxvi. Post collationem contra donatistas. lib. i.
.lxvii. De uidendo deo. lib. i.
.lxviii. De natura et gratia. lib. i.
.lxix. De ciuitate dei. libri .xxii.
.lxx. Ad orosium prbm contra priscillianistas. lib. i.
.lxxi. Ad ieronimum prbm unum de origine anime et alium de sententia iacobi apli. libri .ii.
.lxxii. Ad emeritum donatistarum epm post collationem. lib. i.
.lxxiii. De gestis pelagii. lib. i.
.lxxiiii. De correctione donatistarum. lib. i.
.lxxv. De presentia dei ad dardanum. lib. i.
.lxxvi. Contra pelagium et celestium de gratia xpi et de peccato originali ad albinam pinianum et melaniam. lib. ii.
.lxxvii. Gesta cum emerito donatistarum epo. lib. i.
.lxxviii. Contra sermonem arrianorum. lib. i.
.lxxix. De nuptiis et concupiscentia ad ualerium.
.lxxx. Locutionum. lib. vii.
.lxxxi. Questionum. libri .vii.

beant. Non itaque simus in disputationibus prompti, et in orationibus pigri. Oremus dilectissimi, oremus, ut deus gratie det inimicis nostris maximeque fratribus et dilectoribus nostris intelligere et confiteri post ingentem et ineffabilem ruinam, qua in uno omnes cecidimus, neminem nisi dei gratia liberari, eamque non secundum merita accipientium tanquam debitam reddi, sed tanquam veram gratiam nullis meritis precedentibus gratis dari. Nullum autem est illustrius predestinationis exemplum quam ipse Iesus: unde et in primo libro iam disputavi, et in huius fine commendare delegi. Nullum est inquam illustrius predestinationis exemplum quam ipse mediator. Quisquis fidelis vult eam bene intelligere, attendat ipsum, atque in ipso inveniat et se ipsum. Fidelis inquam qui in eo veram naturam credit et confitetur humanam, id est nostram, quamvis singulariter suscipiente deo verbo in unicum dei filium sublimatam, ita ut qui suscepit et quod suscepit una esset in trinitate persona. Neque enim homine assumpto quaternitas facta est, sed trinitas mansit, assumptione illa ineffabiliter faciente persone unius in deo et homine veritatem. Quoniam non deum tantum dicimus Christum sicut heretici manichei, nec hominem tantum sicut heretici fotiniani, nec ita hominem ut aliquid minus habeat quod humanam certum est pertinere naturam, sive animam, sive in anima mentem rationalem, sive carnem non de femina sumptam sed factam de verbo in carnem converso atque mutato: que omnia tria falsa et vana hereticorum apollinaristarum tres partes varias diversasque fecerunt. Sed dicimus Christum deum verum natum de deo patre sine ullo initio temporis, eundemque hominem verum natum de homine matre certa plenitudine temporis; nec eius humanitatem qua minor est patre minuere aliquid eius divinitati qua equalis est patri. Hoc autem utrumque unus est Christus, qui et secundum deum verissime dixit: Ego et pater unum sumus; et secundum hominem verissime dixit: Pater maior me est.

Qui ergo fecit hunc ex semine David hominem iustum qui nunquam esset iniustus sine ullo merito precedentis voluntatis eius, ipse ex iniustis facit iustos sine ullo merito precedentis voluntatis ipsorum: ut ille caput hi membra sint eius. Qui ergo fecit illum hominem sine ullis eius precedentibus meritis, nullum quod ei dimitteretur vel origine trahere vel voluntate perpetrare peccatum, ipse nullis eorum precedentibus meritis facit credentes in eum quibus dimittit omne peccatum. Qui fecit illum talem ut nunquam habuerit habiturusque sit voluntatem malam, ipse facit in membris eius ex mala voluntate bonam. Et illum ergo et nos predestinavit: quia et in illo ut esset caput nostrum, et in nobis ut eius corpus essemus, non precessura merita nostra sed opera sua futura prescivit. Qui legunt hec, si intelligunt agant gratias deo. Qui autem non intelligunt, orent ut eorum ille sit doctor interior, a cuius facie est scientia et intellectus. Qui vero me errare existimant, etiam atque etiam diligenter que sunt dicta considerent, ne fortassis ipsi errent. Ego autem cum per eos qui meos libros legunt non solum doctior verum etiam et emendatior fio, propitium mihi deum agnosco: et hoc per ecclesie doctores maxime expecto, si et in ipsorum manus venit, dignanturque nosse quod scribo. Explicit liber de bono perseverantie.

In libro retractationum secundo capitulo lxv.

Liber quem prenotavi de .viii. dulcicii questionibus non esset in hoc opere commemorandus inter libros meos, cum sit confectus ex his que a me in aliis ante conscripta sunt, nisi disputationis aliquid a nobis interpositum reperiretur in eo, et uni earum questionum non ex opusculo aliquo alio meo responsionem, sed tunc que potuit occurrere reddidissem. Hic liber sic incipit. Quantum mihi videtur dilectissime fili.

Aurelii augustini yponensis episcopi de .viii. dulcicii questionibus liber incipit.

Quantum michi uidetur
dilectissime fili dulciti
non tardaui respondere
interrogationibus tuis. P
ascha quippe hoc anno
quo dominicum erat
viii. kl. aprilis a cartagine in missas litteras
tue dilectionis accepi. Post aliquot autem dies quos
confestim cartaginem sum profectus. in qua
ciuitate nichil me dictare permisit occupati
onum que ibi non potest deesse nimia multi
tudo. Sed postea quam inde regressus sum: p
actis apud nos quindecim diebus qui me pro
absentiam diuturnam curare alia compule
runt. nam post tres menses redire permissus
sum: rescribere ista non distuli. et abs te mis
sis questionibus que prius per diuersa opuscula
mea iam fuerant pertractata. ex eisdem opus
culis reddere uel solutionem uel certe dispu
tationem meam. Denique illud tantummodo quod
queris quare dixerit dominus. uirum secundum
cor meum. elegi dauid secundum cor meum. cum
ille talia et tanta commiserit. non tractauerim
et quando id exposuerim non potui repperire. et utrum
sit in aliquo libro uel in epistola mea nescio.
eplī quam in utilibus noui disputationis ueteres
seruarem: in hac mea responsione id ultimum
feci. plus uolens ea ponere que habebam in aliis
meis uoluminibus preparata. ut non studio tue
sanctitatis deessem quod michi gratissimum est. non alio
modo dicere eadem cogerer quod michi esset laboriosis
simum ne de aliquo amplius adiuuarer.

Questio prima utrum qui post baptismum peccant
aliquando exeant de gehenna.

Prima itaque tua propositio est utrum aliquando
qui sunt post baptismum peccatores exeant
de gehenna. Aliquorum namque super hoc inquisitionis
diuersa sententia est. respondentium sic ut istorum
primum ita peccatorum finem non habere tormenta. Asse
uerare enim cupiunt tamen peccatum uindictam manere
quam primum. Quibus et perscribitur euangelica illa sen
tentia. quia non exies inde donec reddas nouis
simum quadrantem. Superest quod ut hoc reddi
to possit exire. Creduntur hoc et apostoli diffinitio
to possit exire. Credunt hoc et apostoli diffinitio
nem dicentis. Ipse autem saluus erit sic tamen quasi
per ignem. Sed quoniam alibi legunt inquis et non cog
nouit eam donec peperit quod ita interpretari non
possum: ideo de hoc cupimus fieri certiores. Huc
usque est propositio tua. Cui respondeo ex libro
meo qui inscribitur de fide et operibus. non de hac
re ita locutus sum. Iacobus autem in quosdam tam uehe
menter infestus est. ut qui sapiunt fidem sine operi
bus ualere ad salutem: ut illos etiam demonibus
compararet dicens. Tu credis quoniam unus est deus.
bene facis. Et demones credunt et contremiscunt.
Quid breuius. uerius. uehementiusque dici potuit.
cum et in euangelio legamus hoc dixisse demonia
cum xpistum dei filium confiterentur. et ab illo
corripientur. quod in petri confessione laudatum est.
Quid proderit ait iacobus fratres mei si fidem se quis
dicat habere. opera autem non habeat: Numquid poterit
fides saluare eum: Dicit etiam quia fides
sine operibus mortua est. Quo usque quod falluntur
qui de fide mortua se uitam perpetuam polli
centur: Qua propter diligenter oportet attendere
quomodo accipienda sit pauli apostoli sententia
plane ad intelligendum difficilis ubi ait. Fun
damentum aliud nemo potest ponere preter id
quod positum est. quod est xpistus iesus. Si quis autem super
edificat super fundamentum hoc aurum argentum.
lapides preciosos. ligna fenum. stipulam. uniu
cuiusque opus manifestabitur. Dies enim domini de
clarabit quia in igne reuelabitur. Et uniu
cuiusque opus quale sit: ignis probabit. Si cuius
opus manserit: quod superedificauit mercedem
accipiet. Cuius autem opus arserit: dampnum
patietur. ipse autem saluus erit. sic tamen quasi per ignem.
Quod ita intelligendum putant ut illi inde
autem edificare super hoc fundamentum aurum.
argentum. lapides preciosos. qui fidei que in xpisto
est bona opera adiciunt. illi autem ligna fenum
stipulam. qui cum eandem fidem habeant:
male operantur. Vnde arbitrantur per quasdam pe
nas ignis posse purgari ad salutem percipien

45 The Opened Body as Still Life

Govard Bidloo, *Anatomia Humani Corporis*, 1685

Amsterdam: Published at the expense of the widow of Joannis à Someron, the heirs of Joannis à Dyk, Henry Boom and the widow of Theodore Boom, 1685

Large folio, 480 × 340mm

Provenance: purchased 1812

r17ff QM21.B5

Medical art reached an early height with Vesalius's *De humani corporis fabrica* (1543). Its magnificent large folio plates may have been initially drawn by Titian or his student, and the dense text that accompanied them was Vesalius's astonishing scientific oeuvre, describing systematic, detailed research into the anatomy and workings of the body. His stylized colossi posed in classical landscapes are masterpieces of Renaissance science and art, familiar even to this day.

A century and a half later Govard Bidloo conceived a very different kind of work. An aspiring surgeon who became eminent as a professor and as physician to William of Orange, he was not a discoverer like Vesalius or the great scientific thinkers of his own century. Rather, he set out to make his name with an entirely new set of anatomical dissections, taking advantage of the work of Lower, Willis, Bartholin and other contemporary anatomists. He included the structure of skin, hair and other tissues based on images only recently revealed through the microscope. As illustrator he enlisted one of the foremost painters of the Dutch Golden Age, Gérard de Lairesse. Lairesse was a friend of Rembrandt, who painted his portrait, and, by the time he met Bidloo, already a successful court painter.

Between them, surgeon and painter, they created a work of haunting beauty, detailed and exact in its science, yet with a depth of artistic feeling never found before or since in a work of this kind. The text is spare; the drawings speak for themselves. They tell of osteology, of ligaments, of muscle insertions, of internal organs, but they tell still more about the melancholy beauty of the work they depict. Opened and dissected flesh is shown next to youthful skin, hair, expression, even clothing of the but-recently dead. Pathos is amplified by familiar objects – the pins and cords used for display, a book used as a prop, even a fly that has settled on the edge of a wound. The young woman whose back we see, her hair up, her neck suspended and her limbs propped, looks in death almost as if she were sitting to bathe. We are struck by the sensuality of her curving back, then horrified by the rope around her neck. The juxtaposition of beauty and death is unsettling, as so often in great art, yet what remains is an acute awareness of anatomical dissection in its proper context: the informing of life from death.

Another unnerving series of plates shows the organs and the dead fetus of a woman who died at seven months' gestation. These women are a far cry from the bold Renaissance figures of Vesalius, whose work is literal and commanding. Bidloo and Lairesse leave all to the imagination. Who was the woman whose back we see? How did she die? What life did she lead? Even a hand, so particularly drawn, whose muscles and tendons are displayed so mechanically, makes us wonder: whose hand was it? What used it to do?

There were two editions of *Anatomia Humani Corporis*, the first with Latin text (1685), the second Dutch (1690). The publisher was then persuaded to sell the copper plates in England where, in perhaps the most brazen act of plagiarism in the history of science, the London surgeon William Cowper republished them as his own work, with a new text that nowhere mentions Bidloo, Lairesse or the engraver, Abraham Blooteling. Most of the paintings still exist, preserved in the Bibliothèque de la Faculté de Médecine in Paris, but the copper plates, like the woodcuts of Vesalius, are no more.

Thomas Traill and Kay Redfield Jamison

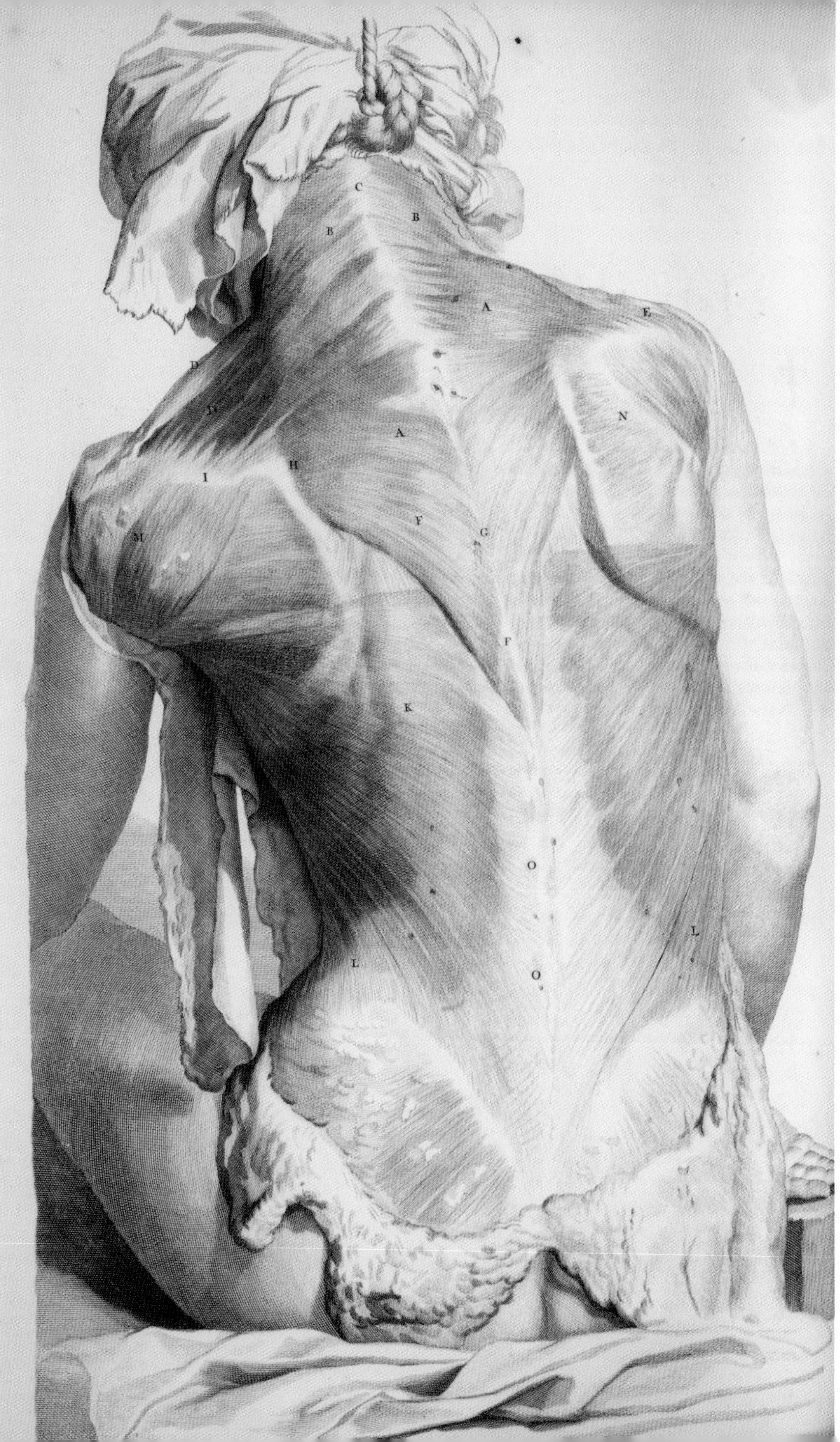
C
B
B
A
E
D
D
N
A
H
I
M
F
G
F
K
O
L
L
O

46 Compare and Contrast

Complutensian Polyglot Bible, 1514–17

Alcalá de Henares: Arnao Guillén de Brocar, 1514–17
Folio, 6 volumes (bound in 3), 356 × 258mm
Provenance: gift of Patrick Young, 1614

The person who invented polyglots should receive a medal. A polyglot is a book, especially a Bible, written in many languages and usually arranged in columns, each containing a different version of the text. This goes back to at least the 3rd century, when the scholar Origen compared the established text of the Old Testament in Greek with the Hebrew Bible and other translations. His example was followed in the 16th century, when humanist scholars sought to recover the most authentic sources of literature, language, philosophy – and the Bible.

Alcalá (Complutum in Latin) is a small city close to Madrid. It is the land of Cervantes, the place where Don Quixote battled against the windmills. It is also the place where Cardinal Francisco Jiménez de Cisneros founded a new university, the predecessor of the University of Madrid, which opened to students in 1508. According to its constitution, the principal object of its theologians was to study the biblical languages, Hebrew, Greek and Latin.

The cardinal's other great project, the 'Complutensian Polyglot', must have started soon after the new university opened its doors. Jiménez assembled a team of renowned scholars and procured ancient manuscripts to enable their studies. The multi-volume work was printed in 1514–17, but had to wait until 1520 for papal approval. The library is the proud owner of a copy of this first edition.

Of the original six parts, four parts comprised the Old Testament, one part the New Testament, and the final part indices and a lexicon. The illustrated page shows the opening words of the Bible. The central column is the Latin Vulgate, the accepted version of the Bible in that period. The left column contains the Greek Septuagint with an interlinear Latin translation. A Greek text was included because Greek translations of the Hebrew Bible went as far back as the 3rd century BC, and Greek was an important language for early Christians and Church leaders. To the right is Hebrew, the language in which most of the Bible was written. At the foot of the page is a Targum, an Aramaic translation of the Hebrew Bible, again with a Latin translation.

Juxtaposing several texts in four languages, two of which were read from right to left, presented considerable typographical difficulty. The problem of keeping the texts in line with each other was solved by the use of repeated space-filling characters in the Hebrew, Aramaic and Latin columns.

With multiple versions of the Bible printed on the same page, comparative work could begin. Scholars could now easily identify the differences between versions and ponder the reasons for them. An example occurs in Leviticus 11:29, which contains words that rarely occur in the Hebrew Bible: weasel, mouse and a great lizard. When translated into Greek the weasel remained a weasel, the mouse remained a mouse, but the great lizard became a crocodile. The Greek specified that this crocodile was living on dry land. It is precisely these kinds of differences that can be recognized at a glance when consulting a polyglot.

Polyglots played a major role in the beginning of critical biblical scholarship. Today, because critical editions of all biblical text versions have not yet been produced, scholars still consult polyglots.

Kristin De Troyer

Trāſla. Grec. lxx. cū interp. latina.

In pricipio fecit deus celum et terrā.
ἐν ἀρχῇ ἐποίησεν ὁ θεὸς τὸν οὐρανὸν καὶ τὴν γῆν. ἡ
at terra erat inuiſibilis ⁊ icōpoſita. et tenebre ſu
δὲ γῆ ἦν ἀόρατος καὶ ἀκατασκεύαστος. καὶ σκότος ἐ-
per abyſſum: et ſpiritus dei ferebatur ſu
πάνω τῆς ἀβύσσου. καὶ πνεῦμα θεοῦ ἐπεφέρετο ἐ-
per aquam. et dixit deus fiat lux. ⁊ fa
πάνω τοῦ ὕδατος. καὶ εἶπεν ὁ θεὸς γενηθήτω φῶς. καὶ ἐ-
cta ē lux. et vidit deus lucē: q bona. et di
γένετο φῶς. καὶ εἶδεν ὁ θεὸς τὸ φῶς, ὅτι καλόν. καὶ διε-
uiſit deus inter lucē: ⁊ inter
χώρισεν ὁ θεὸς ἀναμέσον τοῦ φωτός, καὶ ἀναμέσον τοῦ
tenebras. ⁊ vocauit deus lucē diem: et tene
σκότους. καὶ ἐκάλεσεν ὁ θεὸς τὸ φῶς ἡμέραν, καὶ τὸ σκό-
bras vocauit noctē. et factū ē veſpe: et factū ē
τος ἐκάλεσε νύκτα. καὶ ἐγένετο ἑσπέρα, καὶ ἐγένετο
mane: dies vnus. et dixit deus fiat firmamētū in
πρωΐ, ἡμέρα μία. καὶ εἶπεν ὁ θεὸς γενηθήτω στερέωμα ἐν
medio aque. ⁊ ſit diuidens inter aquā
μέσῳ τοῦ ὕδατος. καὶ ἔστω διαχωρίζον ἀναμέσον ὕδα-
⁊ aquā. ⁊ fecit deus firmamētū. ⁊ di-
τος καὶ ὕδατος. καὶ ἐποίησεν ὁ θεὸς τὸ στερέωμα. καὶ διε-
uiſit deus inter aquam: q̄ erat ſub
χώρισεν ὁ θεὸς ἀναμέσον τοῦ ὕδατος, ὃ ἦν ὑποκάτω τοῦ
firmamēto: et inter aquā: que ſuper
στερεώματος, καὶ ἀναμέσον τοῦ ὕδατος, τοῦ ἐπάνω
firmamētū. et vocauit deus firmamētū ce-
τοῦ στερεώματος. καὶ ἐκάλεσεν ὁ θεὸς τὸ στερέωμα οὐρα-
lum. et vidit deus. q bonū. et factū ē veſpere: ⁊
νόν. καὶ εἶδεν ὁ θεὸς, ὅτι καλόν. καὶ ἐγένετο ἑσπέρα, καὶ
factū ē mane: dies ſecūdus. ⁊ dixit deus cōgre-
ἐγένετο πρωΐ, ἡμέρα δευτέρα. καὶ εἶπεν ὁ θεὸς συναχ-
getur aqua que ſub celo in congrega-
θήτω τὸ ὕδωρ τὸ ὑποκάτω τοῦ οὐρανοῦ εἰς συναγω-
tiōes vnā: et appareat arida. ⁊ factū ē ita. ⁊ cō-
γὴν μίαν, καὶ ὀφθήτω ἡ ξηρά. καὶ ἐγένετο οὕτως. καὶ συ-
gregata ē aqua que ſub celo in cōgre
νήχθη τὸ ὕδωρ τὸ ὑποκάτω τοῦ οὐρανοῦ εἰς τὰς συνα-
gatiōes ſuas: ⁊ apparuit arida. ⁊ vocauit deus ari
γωγὰς αὐτοῦ, καὶ ὤφθη ἡ ξηρά. καὶ ἐκάλεσεν ὁ θεὸς τὴν ξη-
dā: terrā. ⁊ cōgregatiōes aquarū vocauit: ma
ρὰν, γῆν. καὶ τὰ συστήματα τῶν ὑδάτων ἐκάλεσε θα-
ria. et vidit deus: q bonū. et dixit deus ger
λάσσας. καὶ εἶδεν ὁ θεὸς, ὅτι καλόν. καὶ εἶπεν ὁ θεὸς βλα-
minet terra herbā feni ſeminātē ſemē ſm
στησάτω ἡ γῆ βοτάνην χόρτου σπεῖρον σπέρμα κατὰ
genus ⁊ ſcdʒ ſimilitudinē: et lignū pomiferū faciēs
γένος καὶ καθ᾽ ὁμοιότητα, καὶ ξύλον κάρπιμον ποιοῦν
fructū. cuius ſemē ipſius in ipſo ſcdʒ genus ſup
καρπὸν. οὗ τὸ σπέρμα αὐτοῦ ἐν αὐτῷ κατὰ γένος ἐπὶ
terrā. ⁊ factū ē ita. et protulit terra her-
τῆς γῆς. καὶ ἐγένετο οὕτως. καὶ ἐξήνεγκεν ἡ γῆ βοτά-
bā feni ſeminātē ſemē ſm genus ⁊ ſcdʒ ſimi
νην χόρτου σπεῖρον σπέρμα κατὰ γένος καὶ καθ᾽ ὁμοιό-
litudinē: ⁊ lignū pomiferū faciens fructū. cuius ſe
τητα, καὶ ξύλον κάρπιμον ποιοῦν καρπόν. οὗ τὸ σπέρ-
mē eius in ipſo: ſcdʒ genus ſup terrā. et vidit
μα αὐτοῦ ἐν αὐτῷ κατὰ γένος ἐπὶ τῆς γῆς. καὶ εἶδεν

Tranſla. B. Hiero.

.I.

In principio creauit deus celum & terrā. Terra autem erat inanis & vacua: & tenebre erant ſup faciē abyſſi: & ſpiritus dei ferebatur ſuper aquas. Dixitq̧ deus. Fiat lux. Et facta ē lux. Et vidit deus lucem q eſſet bona: & diuiſit lucem a tenebris: appellauitq̧ lucem diē: & tenebras noctem. Factumq̧ eſt veſpe & mane dies vnus. Dixit quoq̧ deus. Fiat firmamentū in medio aquarum: & diuidat aquas ab aquis. Et fecit deus firmamentum. diuiſitq̧ aquas q̄ erant ſub firmamēto ab his que erant ſuper firmamentū. Et factū eſt ita. Vocauitq̧ deus firmamentum celum: & factum eſt veſpe & mane dies ſecundus. Dixit vero deus. Congregentur aque q̄ ſub celo ſunt in locum vnum: & appareat arida. Et factum ē ita. Et vocauit deus aridā terram: cōgregationeſq̧ aquarū appellauit maria. & vidit deus q eſſet bonum: & ait. Germinet terra herbā virētem & faciētē ſemē: & lignum pomiferū faciens fructū iuxta genus ſuū cuius ſemē ī ſemetipſo ſit ſup terrā. Et factū eſt ita. Et ꝓtulit terra herbā virētē & faciētē ſemē iuxta genus ſuū: lignū q̧ faciēs fructū: & hn̄s vnū quodq̧ ſementem ſm ſpēm ſuā. Et vidit

Ter. Heb. Gen. Ca. i.

בראשית ברא אלהים את
השמים ואת הארץ׃ והארץ
היתה תהו ובהו וחשך על פני
תהום ורוח אלהים מרחפת על
פני המים׃ ויאמר אלהים יהי
אור ויהי אור׃ וירא אלהים את
האור כי טוב ויבדל אלהים בין
האור ובין החשך׃ ויקרא אלהים
לאור יום ולחשך קרא לילה
ויהי ערב ויהי בקר יום אחד׃
ויאמר אלהים יהי רקיע בתוך
המים ויהי מבדיל בין מים
למים׃ ויעש אלהים את הרקיע
ויבדל בין המים אשר מתחת
לרקיע ובין המים אשר מעל
לרקיע ויהי כן׃ ויקרא אלהים
לרקיע שמים ויהי ערב ויהי
בקר יום שני׃ ויאמר אלהים
יקוו המים מתחת השמים אל
מקום אחד ותראה היבשה ויהי
כן׃ ויקרא אלהים ליבשה ארץ
ולמקוה המים קרא ימים וירא
אלהים כי טוב׃ ויאמר אלהים
תדשא הארץ דשא עשב מזריע
זרע עץ פרי עשה פרי למינו
אשר זרעו בו על הארץ ויהי
כן׃ ותוצא הארץ דשא עשב
מזריע זרע למינהו ועץ עשה
פרי אשר זרעו בו למינהו וירא

Pritiua. heb.

Ca. i.

ראש
היה תהה בהה
פנה
תהם רחף
אמר היה
ראה
בדל
קרא
רקע
בדל
עשה
שנה
קוה
ראה
קרא
קוה
דשא זרע
פרה היה
יצא

Tranſla. Chal.

בקדמין ברא ייי ית שמיא וית ארעא׃ וארעא הות צדיא וריקניא וחשוכא על
תהומא ורוחא דייי מנשבא על אפי מיא׃ ואמר ייי יהא נהורא והוה נהורא׃ וחזא
ית נהורא ארי טב ואפריש ייי בין נהורא ובין חשוכא׃ וקרא ייי לנהורא יממא
ולחשוכא קרא ליליא והוה רמש והוה צפר יומא חד׃ ואמר ייי יהא רקיעא במצע
מיא ויהא מפריש בין מיא למיא׃ ועבד ייי ית רקיעא ואפריש בין מיא דמלרע
לרקיעא ובין מיא דמלעיל לרקיעא והוה כן׃ וקרא ייי לרקיעא שמיא והוה
רמש והוה צפר יום תנין׃ ואמר ייי יתכנשון מיא מתחות שמיא לאתר חד ותתחזי יבשתא
והוה כן׃ וקרא ייי ליבשתא ארעא ולבית כנישות מיא קרא ימי וחזא ייי ארי
ואמר ייי תדאי ארעא דיתאה עשבא דבר זרעיה מזדרע אילן פרין עביד פרין
לזנוהי דבר זרעיה ביה על ארעא והוה כן׃ ואפיקת ארעא דיתאה עשבא דבר
מזדרע לזנוהי ואילן עביד פרין דבר זרעיה ביה לזנוהי וחזא

Interp. chal.

In principio creauit deus celū ⁊ terrā. Ca. i. Terra aūt erat deſerta ⁊ vacua: ⁊ tenebre ſup faciem abyſſi: ⁊ ſpūs dei inſufflabat ſup faciē aquaꝝ. Et dixit deus. Sit lux: ⁊ fuit lux. ⁊ vidit deus lucē q eſſet bona. Et diuiſit deus inter lucē ⁊ inter tenebras. appellauitq̧ deus lucē diē: ⁊ tenebras vocauit noctē. Et fuit veſpe ⁊ fuit mane dies vnus. Et dixit deus. Sit firmamentū in medio aquaꝝ: ⁊ diuidat inter aquas ⁊ aq̄s. Et fecit deus firmamentū: et diuiſit īter aquas q̄ erant ſubter firmamētuꝫ: ⁊ inter aq̄s q̄ erant ſup firmamentū: ⁊ fuit ita. Et vocauit de⁹ firmamentū celuꝫ. Et fuit veſpe ⁊ fuit mane dies ſcd̄s. Et dixit de⁹. Cōgregētur aque q̄ ſub celo ſunt in locū vnum: ⁊ appareat arida. Et fuit ita. Et vocauit deus aridā terrā: ⁊ locū cōgregationis aquarū appellauit maria. Et vidit de⁹ qd̄ eſſet bonū. Et dixit deus. Germinet terra germinationē herbe cui⁹ filius ſemētis ſeminat: arborēq̧ fructiferā facientē fructus ſm genus ſuū: cuius filius ſemētis in ipſo ſit ſup terrā. Et fuit ita. Et ꝓduxit terra germē herbe cuius filius ſemētis ſeminat ſm genus ſuū: et arborē facientē fructus: cui⁹ filius ſemētis ī ipſo ſm genus ſuū. Et vidit

Pritiua chal.

הוה צדה ריק
נשב הוה
טוב פרש
מצע
פרש ארע
עלה
כנש חזה
טוב
דאה זרע פרה
זנא עבק דאה
זרע

47 An Overwhelming Impression of Luxury

Heures de nostre Dame a l'usaige de Chartres, 1558

Paris: Jacques Kerver, 1558
8vo, 167 × 103mm
Provenance: purchased 2007
Typ FP.B58KH

Books of hours were the most popular type of book in late mediaeval France. They were aimed at the laity and provided a mixture of prayers, psalms and religious texts for each hour of the day. Thousands of handwritten and hand-illustrated volumes were created and sold during the 15th century. With the advent of the presses numerous printed versions were produced with specific liturgies for the various bishoprics.

This edition was printed for the cathedral city of Chartres, situated some 60 miles to the southwest of Paris, for Jacques Kerver. The Kerver dynasty had made such popular religious books their speciality and dominated that niche with high-quality imprints that they distributed throughout France.

Though there were numerous editions of books of hours throughout the 16th century, surviving copies are rare. These volumes were subject to heavy daily usage and, though some were printed on vellum (an expensive but robust replacement for paper), many survive only as fragments. The St Andrews copy of the hours for the use of Chartres is not only complete, it is also the only known surviving copy of this edition. Until the library acquired the volume in 2007, this edition remained completely unknown to scholars.

Books of hours were prestigious objects that were richly illustrated with complex printed images, sometimes painted over to resemble the illuminated manuscripts they replaced. This edition contains no fewer than 60 large illustrations, featuring not only pious iconography of the holy family, but also traditional favorites such as the *Danse Macabre*. The first 28 pages form a religious calendar, with seasonal non-religious imagery for each month containing the relevant zodiacal symbolism.

But if the rarity of the edition and the richness of the illustrations make the book valuable, this volume is all the more remarkable because of the beauty of its binding. The ornate gold-tooled, interlaced motif was typical of Parisian bookbinding of the second half of the 16th century. It combines some of the most distinctive features of French Renaissance decorative art with the use of gold to give an overwhelming impression of luxury.

Beyond its artistic value, the volume is also of great interest for what it tell us about Catholicism when it was printed. If the layout of the hours had gradually changed over the decades, the 16th-century printers were keen to maintain a degree of resemblance to the manuscript volumes they replaced. This desire to be associated with the manuscript tradition is demonstrated here by the use of gothic type enhanced by the use of both red and black ink. During the 1540s and 1550s the use of the more fashionable Roman and italic types had all but completely supplanted the gothic typefaces. But gothic type was much closer to 16th-century handwriting, and it would have reminded readers of the longstanding traditions represented by the Catholic Church – an important feature in a period where the Church was increasingly under threat from the rise of French Calvinism.

Malcolm Walsby

Februarius.

Les six dapres resemblent a Feburier
En fin duquel commence le printemps
Car lesprit se ouure prest a enseigner
Et doulx deuient lenfant quant a douze ans.

Ligna cremo.

KL Februarius habet dies. xxviii. Luna. xxix. Et quando est bissextus habet dies. xxix. Luna. xxx.

	d	Ignatii epi	xvi	d	Faustini
xi	e	Purifi. marie		e	Iuliane vir.
xix	f	Blasii epi	xv	f	
viii	g	Gilberti	iiii	g	Simeonis
	A	Agathe virg.		A	
xvi	b	Vedasti	xii	b	Eustachii
v	c		i	c	
	d			d	Cathe. petri
xiii	e	Apollonie	ix	e	Vigilia
ii	f	Scolastice.		f	Mathie apo.
	g	Soteris	xvii	g	
x	A	Eulalie	vi	A	
	b			b	Honorini
xviii	c	Valentini.	xiiii	c	Iustini

Au/chan/de/lier/a/ga/the/beut/
Mais/le/vin/si/fort/les/meut/
Quil/tu/a/pres/dauf/si/
Pier/res/mat/thias/auf/si.

Piscis frigidum & humidum/ signum indifferens.

Piscis habens lunam/noli curare podagram.

Tutus iter carpis/fit potio sumpta salubris.
Aurum debet emi/sponse sponsus sociari.

Ure igne sancti spiritus renes nostros & cor nostrum domine: vt tibi casto corpore seruiamus, & mundo corde placeamus. Per christum. Oratio.

Gratiam tuam quesumus domine mentibus nostris infunde: vt qui angelo nunciante christi filij tui incarnationem cognouimus, per passionem eius et crucem ad resurrectionis gloriam perducamur. Per. Oratio.

Ecclesiam tuam quesumus domine benignus illustra: vt beati Johannis apostoli tui et euangeliste illuminata doctrinis ad dona perueniat sempiterna. Per dominum nostrū iesum christum filium tuum. Qui tecum viuit & regnat deus. Per omnia secula seculorum. Amen.

Ad cōpletoriū De sancta cruce.

A complie enuiron la nuyt
Dedens le sepulchre fut mys
Oing de baulme, sans aucū bruyt
Par les mains de ses bons amys

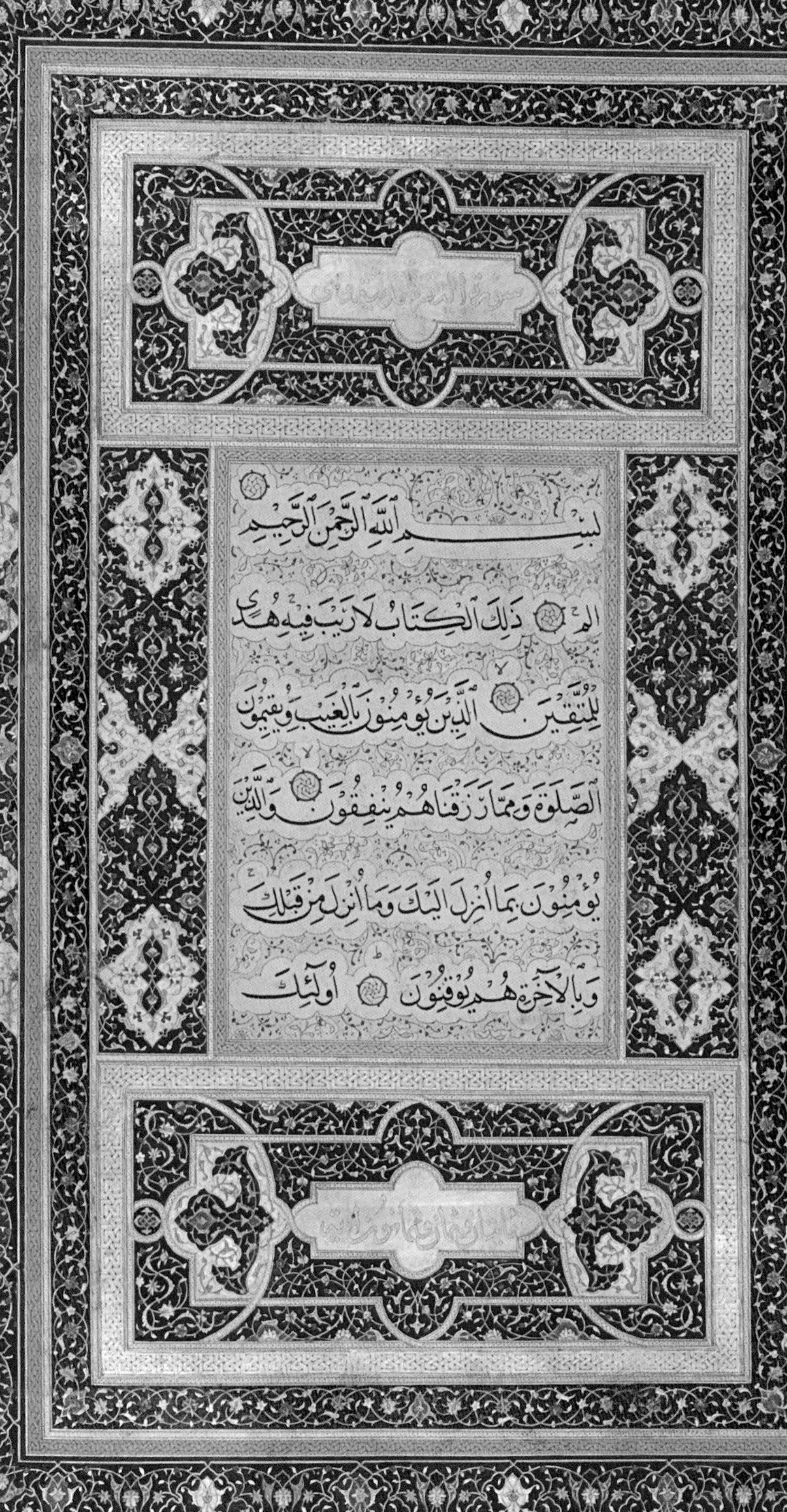

سورة البقرة
بسم الله الرحمن الرحيم
الم ذلك الكتاب لا ريب فيه هدى
للمتقين الذين يؤمنون بالغيب ويقيمون
الصلوة ومما رزقناهم ينفقون والذين
يؤمنون بما انزل اليك وما انزل من قبلك
وبالآخرة هم يوقنون اولئك

48 The Devotion of the Calligrapher

Timurid Qur'an, AH845/AD1441–2

Paper, 344 × 235mm, in original gold-tooled leather binding
Provenance: from the library of Tipu Sultan (Mysore, India); presented by the East India Company, 1806
ms19(O)

Traditional Islamic art intertwines religion with a love of beauty, but it does so within the boundaries of Islamic law, which prohibits the representation of the human form. These confines led artisans to develop highly intricate geometric patterns and to formulate a variety of Arabic scripts. Within Islamic societies, a copy of the Qur'an is one of the most revered and treasured possessions, whether it be written on plain paper in a simple script or an illuminated manuscript destined for a royal patron, as with this Timurid Qur'an.

The Timurid dynasty began in the late 14th century under the leadership of the Turco-Mongol conqueror Timur, known through European literature as Tamerlane. At their zenith, Timur's domains extended from Turkey to the western mountains of China and south into India. Once the vast empire had been subjugated, Timur's heirs turned instead to cultural development, many of them becoming patrons of architecture, fine arts and the written word. A dedication note on the cover states that this manuscript was written in AD 1441–2 (AH845) by a scribe identified as Muhammad Mu'min ibn Abdallah al-Muwarid, for Sultan Abu Said Shuja ad-Din Bahadur Khan, one of Timur's grandsons who ruled Transoxiana from *c.*1457 to 1469.

Although in many ways typical of royal manuscripts of this era, it is unusually complete and stunningly well preserved, making it one of the prime remaining examples of a Timurid Qur'an. Skilled Qur'anic calligraphers paid particular detail to the embellishment of the first page, since it contained the first sura (chapter) of the Qur'an. Other areas of ornamentation include the side margins and headers, especially the pages where new suras commence. The geometric patterns in the manuscript are similar to those seen in the architecture of this era, and the vivid colours are typical of Timurid manuscripts, particularly the dark blue background with a gold and red floral motif used in the sura headings. Medallions are positioned throughout the work in a variety of colours and styles. The script is a combination of *naskhi* in the main text and *rayhani* in the headings and enlarged quotations. Comments in the margins by scholars who used this manuscript include legal interpretations, indications for recitation and personal observations.

The devotion of the calligrapher both to his religion and to his art cannot fail to be admired, even by those who do not understand Arabic, in this strikingly beautiful manuscript.

J. Tia Wheeler

في تكذيب والله من ورائهم محيط بل هو قرآن مجيد
بسم الله الرحمن الرحيم
والسماء والطارق وما ادريك ما الطارق النجم الثاقب
من بين الصلب والترائب انه على رجعه لقادر يوم تبلى السرائر
والسماء ذات الرجع والارض ذات الصدع انه لقول فصل
انهم يكيدون كيدا واكيد كيدا
والسماء والطارق

nechsten cap. gelert hab. Darnach werden sie gedigeriert/fermentiert/vnd distilliert in balneo marie/so der mon ist im wid'/so er fry ist von infortunis mit freuntlichem aspect etlich fortun Jouis oder veneris. Deß gleichē sol der mon genumē werden so er ist im wider mit aspect fortune. Du magst auch wol darüber thůn Aqua vite in der vile / oder an stat des wassers wie oben daruon geschreiben stot.

☞ Was virtutes vñ krafft habē ist Aurea Alexandrina/hab ich oben gezeigt.

☞ Virtutes vnd krafft Dya musci

☞ Virtutes vnd krafft Dya Anthos.

☞ Virtutes vnd krafft Dya Ambra.

☞ Virtutes vñ confectio. Anacardine.

Dise alle findestu obē iedes an seinem ort.

Was virtutes vñ kraft

habē ist Dya Macis/so mā darzů thůtt

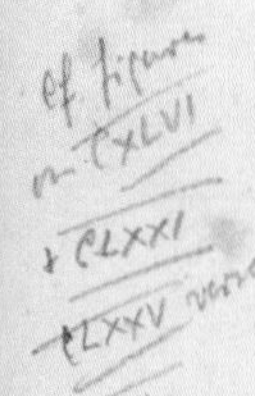

Muscū/das ist bisem/ welches genant ist Dya macis cū musco/ wil ich hie ercleren vß der ler des Antidotarii Serapionis in dem.xx. Capitel.

Dia macis den nāmē empfahet vō muscat blůt dz ist macis / ist vast stercken dz hertz vñ dz hirn sunderlich so man darzů thůn ist muscū/ vnd ist auch gůt für die blůtrůr/vnd da ein mensch begert zů stůl gon vñ doch nit mag/genāt Tenasmon vñ allen flüssen hilfft es / vnd stercket den kalten magen/ vnd ist gůt für wind in dē buch vō böser teuwung/ vñ ist

Was virtutes vñ kraft

an im haben ist Dya Rodon Julii.

Dia Rodon Julii Cesaris imperatoris/dē namē es hat vō Keiser Julio/ vō dē es funden ward/ vnd genant ist ein mechtige artznei für denn bösen vnnd kychenden athem / für denn hůsten von der kal

49 Syrupus, Wassers, Confectios and Pillules

Hieronymus Brunschwig, *Das Buch zu Distillieren*, 1519

Strasburg: Johann Grüninger, 1519

Folio, 301 × 205mm

Provenance: purchased for the university by John Read, Professor of Chemistry (1923–63); transferred to the custody of the library, 1989

This book is widely and rather unattractively known as the *Gross Distillierbuch*, a title that little reflects its extraordinary contents. Like the first edition of 1512, this 1519 edition of the text is illustrated with superb woodcuts. Described elsewhere as 'the first great work on chemistry ever published', the volume is a magnificent text covering all that was known of pharmacology and the therapeutic uses of plants in the 16th century, and it was to be influential for at least another 300 years.

It first offers practical advice on chemical distillation processes to produce essential oil- or water-based extracts from plants, followed by a survey of preparations – *syrupus*, *wassers*, *confectios* and *pillules* – that are thought efficacious for all human ailments. Here you can find remedies for red or black cholera, for melancholy or pestilence, for *alle würme* and even for a 'stopped-up liver'. A treatment of alopecia (hair loss) has been particularly well-thumbed and annotated, perhaps by a previous bald male owner, though it requires an astonishing 34 ingredients.

Since Brunschwig was himself a surgeon, we are also treated to sections on anatomy and surgery, beautifully illustrated with blood-lettings, dissections and scenes from sickbeds. Sadly, this volume does not include botanical illustrations, though in later editions many were added.

Within the history of science and medicine, Brunschwig's work was important in consolidating the use of traditional herbal remedies (many in use since Galen's time some 14 centuries earlier) and of newly discovered plant-based treatments for illness and wounds. This proved crucial at a time when Paracelsus and his followers were promoting 'reformed' medical preparations based on metals such as mercury, arsenic and antimony, linked to alchemical traditions. It was, thankfully, the herbal tradition that effectively won this battle. We know now that the strange compounds found in plants are no accident, having been honed by natural selection for their protective effects as feeding deterrents or toxins acting against herbivorous insects and mammals. Having those roles in the plants, it is no surprise that the chemicals in Brunschwig's distillates do affect human health. Today we can explain why the pine resin or cedar oil, myrrh or laudanum, saffron or liquorice, cinnamon or ginger that recur in Brunschwig's recipes do indeed have a therapeutic effect at safe dosages (though we might struggle with 'dragon's blood', 'long pepper' or 'grains of paradise' until our wildflower book reveals these as folk names for quite normal plants).

A vast number of modern treatments are still based on plant products, from simple aspirin to the potent anti-cancer drugs taxol (from yew) and vinblastine (from periwinkle). It would surely have pleased Brunschwig to know that pharmaceutical companies nowadays help to preserve the biodiversity of rainforest flora which, as we explore it further, will provide the raw materials for new, life-saving ethnobotanical drugs.

Pat Willmer

50 Feasting, Fighting and Football

Acta Facultatis Artium, 1413–1588, 1615–1728

Paper, 288 × 205mm, in 15th-century binding
Provenance: working record of the Faculty of Arts
UYUY411/1

The *Acta Facultatis Artium* is the first minute book of the Faculty of Arts of the University of St Andrews. Written in Latin, it records matters discussed in the general congregations of faculty members, which were held regularly during each year from 1413 to 1588, and concludes with a list of annual elections of officials, 1615–1728. The *Acta* is a key part of the muniment collection and essential evidence for the early history of the university. Most of the institution's mediaeval records relate primarily to lands, titles, privileges and regulations. The *Acta*, however, enhances our understanding of these formal aspects of the corporate history of the university, while also shedding light on the daily workings of the faculty and its engagement with the wider university and the world beyond.

The *Acta* was compiled to keep a functional, working record of ongoing business. In addition to regulating routine matters such as teaching, exams, graduation, finances and discipline, it records the appointment of faculty members and lists the scholars who attained bachelors or masters degrees in Arts in a given year. Similar documentation no longer exists for the other faculties, Theology and Canon Law, which were known to have been operating in mediaeval St Andrews. As the only contemporary and almost continuous record of proceedings dating from the foundation of the university and as one of the most extensive and finest examples of its type surviving from any mediaeval university, the *Acta* is invaluable.

Documentation of the mundane often provides great insight into practical and intellectual concerns. Even the way in which the date is recorded in these early minutes has evidential value. It outlines the faculty's calendar and, because it frequently names the place in which the meeting was held, illustrates the young university's initial dependence on buildings within the priory for the conduct of official business. Financial entries offer an understanding not only of the ever-thorny issue of tuition fees but also the faculty's strategies for enduring 'hard times': restricting expenditure on feasting and granting dispensation from teaching obligations for a suitable sum. Frequent revisiting of curricular policy reveals that the correct approach to philosophy was so hotly contested that it could even induce masters to quit St Andrews and incite physical violence against the dean of the faculty. Indeed, the *Acta* provides the main evidence of serious rivalry between the Faculty of Arts and St Salvator's College in the 15th century. In this context, periodic attempts to prohibit members from carrying weapons and recommendations to dispense corporal punishment are unsurprising. Further social commentary is provided in regulations imposed on dress, board and expenditure, and the prohibition of cock-fighting and football.

Various minutes trace the engagement of the faculty and its members with the wider political and religious preoccupations of the period and the impact of such on university affairs. Disruptions to the academic timetable coincided with political turmoil in Scotland, such as James II's action against the Douglas family and the aftermath of the battle of Flodden. The *Acta* also highlights the influential role of the Faculty of Arts in Scotland's decision to abandon its support of the university's benefactor, Benedict XIII in 1418, and later, between 1431 and 1449, certain St Andrews alumni recorded in the *Acta* joined the schismatic Council of Basle, which questioned the absolute authority of the pope. In tracing the fluctuating fortunes of the faculty from its beginnings as a displaced community of scholars seeking to buttress the Catholic Church, to its efforts to survive and adapt to the altered religious climate of post-Reformation Scotland, the *Acta* is a highly unusual example of an early European university record.

Isla Woodman

Nova bacalarii Anno domini m° iiii° xvij

...as de Kethe
...mus de Lawad
...tus forestar
...s petryne
...tinus Kethe
...Edwardus galbraythe
...nus bowar
...de Kedas
...ce Days
...lis thortown

[C]ongregacione facultatis tenta xvij° die februarii in capella sancti [illegible] a maiori parte conclusum fuit [illegible] doctrina Alberti adhuc non legitur in isto studio set Buridani Item quod bidellus habeat de quolibet [illegible] laris disputaturis octo denarios

[C]ongregacione facultatis tenta apud sanctum leonardum [illegible] die mensis augusti fuit conclusum quod subtraccio [illegible] est obediencie a petro de luna quondam nuncupato benedicto et quilibet magister facultatis [illegible] [illegible] subtraccionem ab eo obedienciam et obedit martino/ Deinde [illegible] [illegible] ad hoc [illegible] [illegible] tanto consilio coram gubernatore et tribus statibus regni ex parte facultatis [illegible] ad inducendum [illegible] gubernatorem et totum consilium ad solempnem celebrandam subtraccionem a dicto petro de luna et [illegible] declarandam obedienciam catholice [illegible] pro domino nostro martino quinto Item quod solempnitas [illegible] prorogaretur usque ad generale consilium ob reverencia domini gubernatoris et tocius regni [illegible] Et in casu quo gubernator non velit facere subtraccionem [illegible] set velit [illegible] in obediencia [illegible] [illegible] sibi [illegible] ut quidam dicit tunc facultas solempnizabit subtraccionem [illegible] Item quod [illegible] [illegible] aliquis [illegible] et notabilis aurifaber eciam expensis facultatis si opereat ad [illegible] [illegible] ut veniat cum virga et [illegible] eam in ista civitate et si non velit quod ipse mittat virgam cum [illegible] [illegible] [illegible] sibi [illegible] pro opere suo/ Item quod [illegible] bidellus [illegible] pro isto anno [illegible] [illegible] [illegible] sexaginta solidos [illegible] alias sibi [illegible]

[I]n congregacione tenta in scolis theologie xviij° die octobris conclusit facultas quod [illegible] [illegible] [illegible] [illegible] [illegible] non graduati [illegible] magistri [illegible] [illegible] [illegible] in deliberacionibus [illegible] [illegible] [illegible] [illegible] [illegible] [illegible] de pecuniis [illegible] facultatis et sibi [illegible] [illegible] [illegible] [illegible] magistrorum [illegible] in facultate [illegible] pro rectore [illegible] expensis facultatis in [illegible] [illegible] [illegible] [illegible] de [illegible] et benevolencia facultatis habeat [illegible]

Bernardus [illegible] collegii anni supradicti viz xix die mensis decembris

Jacobus Kynninmonth
Alexander Kynninmonth
Georgius Blair
Bernardus Crawfurd
David Sibbald
Patricius Jonstoun

Acta venerabilis et magne speculationis viri magistri Thome Ramsay rectoris de Kenbak decani facultatis artium et anno etc quingentesimo decimo

Congregatione facultatis artium tenta in novis scolis [illegible]
Primo die mensis martii pro electione novi decani quia facul
tas artium viduata seu orbata erat capite per mortem nobilis
magistri Ade Quhytlaw decani electi anno etc sexto quarto die me[nsis]
novembris in qua congregatione elegerunt in decanum magne scien[tie]
virum magistrum Thomam Ramsay rectorem de Kenbak Et in eadem congre
gatione facultas dedit decem assessores ad consulendum decan[um]
[in] agendis pro anno futuro viz magistros Hugonem Spens praeposit[um]
eiusdem collegii Sancti Salvatoris ac officialem Sanctiandree principal[em]
Johannem Burel rectorem de Dunnino Johannem Maitland
subdecanum rossensem Karolum Fodringhame rectorem de [illegible]
Walterum [illegible] rectorem de Ellem Robertum Dawsone Petrum [illegible]
Ramsay Johannem [illegible] cum potestate convocandi alios in absen[tia]
decanum etc.

Congregatione facultatis artium tenta in novis scolis [illegible]
Primo ebdomade quadragesime pro electione temptatorum anno
etc [illegible] In qua congregatione facultas elegit [illegible] tempta
tores viz magistros Johannem Dykesonne et Johannem Gard[ner]
pro regentibus Martinum Balfour et Johannem [illegible] pro
ad temptandum seu examinandum studentes electi anni Et admissi
intrantes ad temptandum et determinandum [illegible] ad respondendum
[illegible] et iurati ut moris est [illegible] erat [illegible]
[illegible] facultatis [illegible] respondet in collegio [illegible]
[illegible] [illegible] [illegible]

[C]ongregatione facult[at]is artium tenta in monasterio Sancti Leonardi [illegible] die mensis [illegible] Anno domini ut supra
[I]n qua congregatione facultas elegit distributores viz magistros [illegible] Ramsay Johannem Gardnare
[illegible] pro festo beati Johannis evangeliste

Nomina Incorporatorum anno [illegible] vi[o]

[Jac]obus Thornton
[An]dreas Ramsay
[Wi]llelmus Sinclar
[T]homas Cunyngham
[Ro]bertus Murray
[illegible] Zolbury
[Ro]bertus Thomson
[R]obertus Makalpe
[illegible] Scot
[illegible] Neilstoun
[Ro]bertus Fyfe
[Rob]ertus Neddrury
[illegible] Gray

Continuatio magistri Thome Ramsay rectoris
de Kenbak in officio decani facultatis
Artium Anno domini millesimo quingentesimo xi

[illegible] die mensis Novembris anno domini millesimo quingentesimo xi in monasterio Sancti
[Leo]nardi facultas continuavit dominum magistrum Thomam Ramsay in decanum
facultatis artium et dedit aliquos assessores pro novis statutis ad consulendum
decanum pro futuro viz magistros Hugonem Spens domini prepositum de pla[illegible]
[illegible] David Spens rectorem de Flisk Johannem Maitland magistrum
[illegible] Jacobum Walter petrum capellanum Robertum Dauson
[illegible] [illegible] alios [illegible] ~~[illegible]~~
~~[illegible] [illegible] magistri Gilberti [illegible] clarc [illegible]~~

Index

The index is selective, and does not as a matter of course include the publication and provenance information provided at the head of each article. References in bold figures are to the Treasure number; others are to pages within the preliminary and ancillary sections. At the end is a guide to the Treasures arranged chronologically within each collection area.

Platycercus Cyanogenys, *from John Gould,* Birds of Australia. Supplement *(London: published by the author, 1869). rff QL693.G7*

Initial from Pseudo-Augustine, Sermones ad fratres in eremo *(Italy, 14th century).* *msBR65.A9S2*

Lacquered binding of Qur'an *(Persia, 1851). ms22(O)*

Detail from panel-stamped binding dated 1488. From Gregory, Moralia in Job *(Paris: Ulrich Gering and Berthold Rembolt, 1495). Typ FPA95GG*

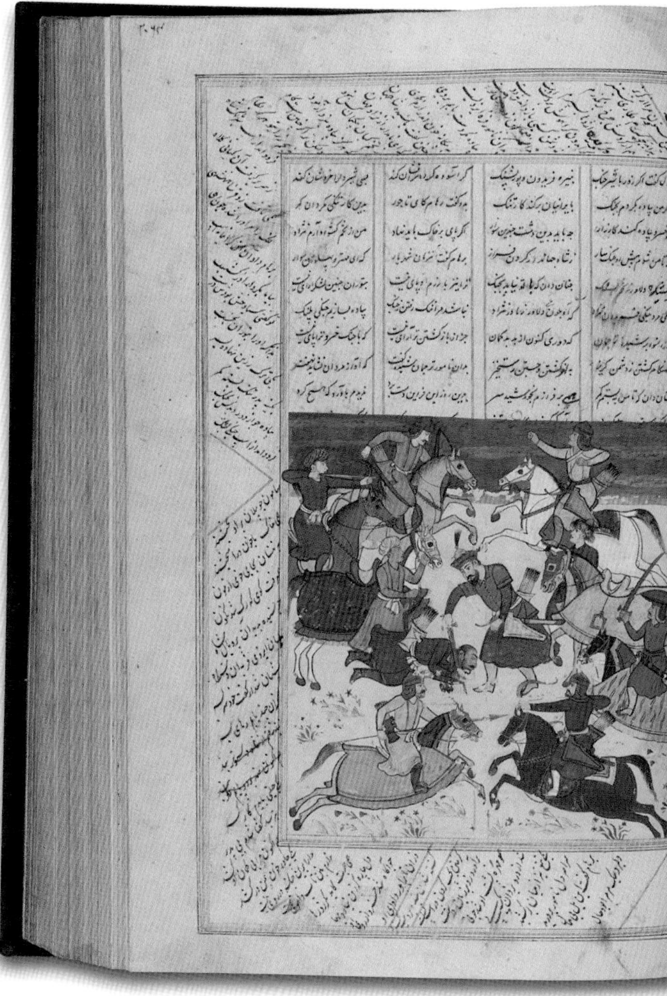

Shah Namah (Book of Kings) *by Firdausi (Persia, 1605). ms28(O)*

The earliest muniment: a charter by John, son of Michael the clerk, granting alms for church lighting (1215). UYSL110/PW/3

Treasures by material type and date

(numbers refer to Treasures)

for for for. fo. clxxiiii. a, l. xi, or for thair. fo, clxxxvi, a, l, v. damna for damnatioun. fo, cliii, a, l, ix, eftir yis word zour, eik that and nocht zour. fo, cliiii, b, l. iiii. that is say, for that is to say. fo, clxxxviii, a, l. xxviii, coast for craft. All uthir faultis, other committit be negligens as thir afore collectit, or be imperfectioun of the prent, the lettir nocht beand fullily fillit with ynk or nocht set in euin & rycht order, ane gentil reader may esely persaif, and thairfor suld reid thame as weil as he can in the best maner.

FINIS.

Prentit at sanct Androus, be the command and expēsis of the maist reuerend father in God, Iohne Archbischop of sanct Androus, and primat of ye hail kirk of Scotland, the xxix. day of August, the zeir of our Lord M.D.lii.